THE 60 SECOND ENCYCLOPEDIA

THE
60 SECOND
ENCYCLOPEDIA

The most amazing things ever done in a single minute!

BY MICHAEL J. ROSEN

WORKMAN PUBLISHING

The author wishes to thank several individuals who spent no small amount of time helping to locate and organize the information here: my friend Douglas Zullo and four generous interns from Denison University—Catherine Stewart, Laura Parker, Meghan Vesper, and Kara Oakleaf. Minute by minute, there's also been the less technical commiseration and support of Mimi Chenfeld and Mark Svede. Finally, appreciation is extended to the team at Workman Publishing, who worked over-and-overtime on this book.

Copyright © 2005 Michael J. Rosen

Illustrations by Elwood Smith
Book and cover design by Janet Parker

Library of Congress Cataloging-in-Publication Data
Rosen, Michael J;, 1954–
The 60-second encyclopedia / by Michael J. Rosen ; illustrations by Elwood Smith.
p. cm.
ISBN-13: 978-0-7611-2902-8;   ISBN-10: 0-7611-2902-2   (alk. paper)
1. Children's encyclopedias and dictionaries. 2. Curiosities and wonders—Juvenile literature.
3. Time—Miscellanea—Juvenile literature. I. Title: Sixty-second encyclopedia.
II. Smith, Elwood H., 1941– ill. III. title

AG6.R67 2005
031—dc22   2004057818

Workman books are available at special discounts when purchased in bulk for premiums and sales promotions as well as for fund-raising or educational use. Special editions can also be created to specification. For details, contact the Special Sales Director at the address below.

Workman Publishing Company, Inc.
708 Broadway
New York, NY 10003-9555
www.workman.com

Printed in China
First printing May 2005
10 9 8 7 6 5 4 3 2 1

"Just a Minute There"

Maybe you think that minutes are hardly worth 306 pages. It's true that minutes are small units of measurement that we take for granted—sort of like pennies. You can't really buy much with pennies unless you save up a lot of them, and minutes don't seem to matter unless you add them up into hours or days.

But minutes are incredibly important! They may fly by, but every minute is jam-packed with amazing things going on—in your body, your house, your backyard, and your world!

Did you ever notice how important minutes are in the movies? And not simply because a single minute of filmmaking can easily cost a cool $1 million. In action films, doesn't it always come down to the last one minute when the bomb's ticking timer or the alien invaders or the evil killer is finally stopped and catastrophe is avoided?

Minutes save the day! Not just "last minutes" in blockbuster movies, but all minutes, everywhere. They "save" your day from the disaster of being late to class or the evil of not knowing what time the train is leaving the station. It's the mission of minutes— all 525,600 that make up a year—to help us in thousands of ways.

Minutes allow you to...

● meet up with your friends at a designated time and place, like "2:40 in front of the movie theater."

● meet up with your car ride home at the correct time so you're not stuck at that movie theater.

● arrive on time to school, to a concert, or to an airplane that's taking you on a fabulous vacation.

● time how fast you run or swim in a race, and regulate your soccer quarters and hockey periods.

● bake cookies or boil an egg or microwave popcorn so that it tastes delicious.

And those are just a very few things that minutes can do (hands tied behind their backs!).

The Sands of Time

This book comes with a minute glass, and how swell is that! This sandglass is made so that when all the sand flows from one half to the other, one minute will have passed. To give you an idea of where your "sands of time" fit into the bigger picture, think of this: There are:

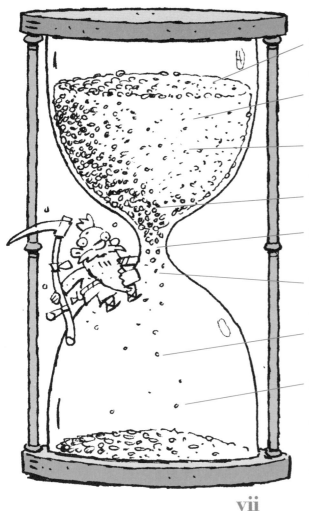

MILLENIUM
5,259,600,000 minutes in a millennium
(1000 years)

CENTURY
52,596,000 minutes in a century
(100 years)

DECADE
5,259,600 minutes in a decade
(10 years)

YEAR
525,600 minutes in a year (365 days)*

MONTH
43,200 minutes in a 30-day month or
44,640 minutes in a 31-day month.**

WEEK
10,080 minutes in a week
(along with 7 days)

DAY
1,440 minutes in a day
(as well as 24 hours)

HOUR
60 minutes in an hour

*plus an extra 1440 minutes every
Leap Year
**February has 40,320 minutes in its
28 days; in leap year, it has 29 days
and 41,760 minutes.

Time Out

The minutes listed in this book are facts and statistics; they're accurate on paper, but actual situations may be different. The cheetah speed listed on page 164 is 1.6 miles per minute because that's the top speed measured by scientists. But cheetahs spend more of their time resting, not sprinting! And some cheetahs are slower.

Some of the facts in this book are based on averages of a wide range of numbers. Your own heartbeat could be a little faster or slower than the resting heart rate on page 205, and that's perfectly fine! Other statistics are based on numbers that are constantly changing, like prices, the U.S. population, food consumption, and so on.

So when you read about a minute's worth of cheetahs or heartbeats or anything else, remember that while the statistics in this book are true, they're not the *whole* truth.

Time Trials

Throughout the pages of this encyclopedia are fun challenges, games, and activities that last for just 60 seconds. They're called "Get Out Your Minute Glass," and they're all "tests of time" that you can do with your sandglass. Here's one to start you off:

Feel the Minute!

Can you "sense" how long a minute is without looking at a clock? Hand someone else your timer. Close your eyes as soon as your friend tells you the timer's started. **After you think 60 seconds has passed, say "One minute!" and open your eyes.** How close were you?

If you're way off, try counting 60 seconds out loud. The traditional way is by reciting, "1 one thousand, 2 one thousand, 3 one thousand . . . ," all the way to "60 one thousand."

You can also use a watch with a second hand, and test yourself. Keep practicing. Does your ability to feel a minute improve if you train yourself?

Bonus: Use your minute glass to invent your own tests. Measure how many times your hamster spins the wheel in its cage in a minute, how frequently a baby laughs, whether someone can drink an entire glass of water in 60 seconds. . . . The possibilities are endless!

Table of Contents

THE 60-SECOND ENCYCLOPEDIA

Part 2: Time Is Money!

Part 3:
It's Feeding Time!

Part 4: Traveling at the Speed of Life

Part 5: Up, Down and All Around

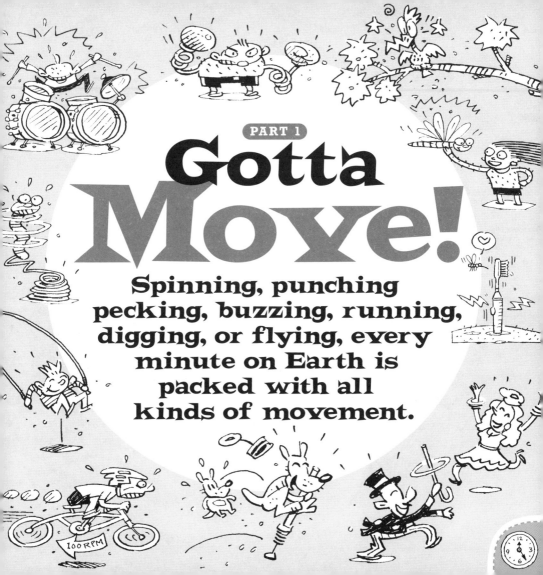

PART 1

Gotta Move!

Spinning, punching pecking, buzzing, running, digging, or flying, every minute on Earth is packed with all kinds of movement.

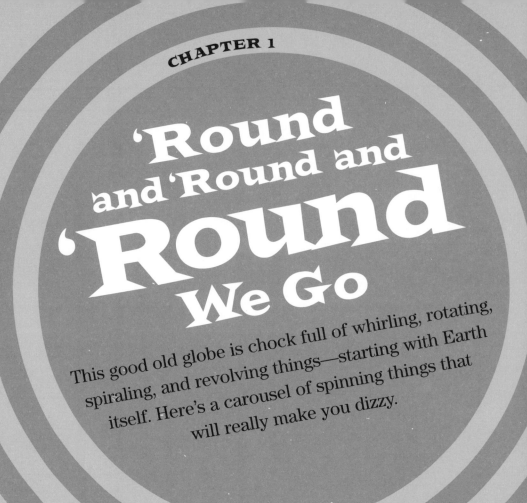

CHAPTER 1

'Round and 'Round and 'Round We Go

This good old globe is chock full of whirling, rotating, spiraling, and revolving things—starting with Earth itself. Here's a carousel of spinning things that will really make you dizzy.

One
60-second lap

The minute hand on your watch makes 1 full revolution in a minute. Of course! That's its job!

One "revolution" is when something makes one complete circle. For instance, when you ride a carousel at the amusement park, your prancing pony makes 2 to 5 revolutions in a minute.

3

THE 60-SECOND ENCYCLOPEDIA

46
silkworm spins

The silkworm is a caterpillar that spends 3 days spinning its cocoon. In 1 minute, it whirls around 46 times and draws up to 1 foot of silk from its body, which humans use to make silk clothing.

How do humans compare? Wendy Moorby can knit over 80 stitches per minute. But she pulls her stitches from a ball of yarn . . . not from her body!

It takes
110 silkworms to make
enough silk for
just one tie!

4
THE 60-SECOND ENCYCLOPEDIA

Check out Ian's Olympic-winning swim speed on page 218.

IN A MINUTE OF SWIMMING . . .

69

swim strokes

Ian Thorpe is one of the world's fastest freestyle swimmers. His arms take about 69 strokes per minute.

You can count your own swim strokes too. It's best to leave your minute glass on the deck though. Add up the number of strokes your arms take in a minute of freestyle, backstroke, breaststroke, and butterfly— which swim style uses the fewest strokes?

5

48
championship cartwheels

The record-holding cartwheeler, Brianna Schroeder, completed 48 cartwheels (each one's a full revolution) in a single minute, which is 1 cartwheel every 1¼ seconds.

Brianna rotates faster than some windmills! On a slow day, a modern windmill's blades spin only 20 times per minute. (When the wind picks up, they're much faster.)

Tumbling Time

This time trial requires plenty of space. To avoid any breakage—as in bones and furniture—try this one in a grassy yard, rec room, or gym.

Take out your minute glass and see how many somersaults you can turn in 60 seconds. And if you aren't too dizzy, see how many cartwheels you can accomplish in a minute too. Do be careful—no extra points for bonking your head.

Cartwheels and somersaults are two ways your body makes one full revolution. There are also front flips and backflips and lots of other, trickier gymnastic moves, as well as just plain rolling down a hill.

GET OUT YOUR MINUTE GLASS

7

100
bicycling cycles

Cyclist Lance Armstrong, who has repeatedly won the
Tour de France (the biggest bicycle race in the universe),
pedals an average 100 revolutions in one minute.

Lance could out-pedal
a ceiling fan . . . but
only on its lowest
setting. And that's why
we don't use bicycles to
cool the house!

270
skating spins

Top figure skater Lucinda Ruh is the "Queen of Spin," able to turn 270 times on the ice in a single minute.

Which top figure skaters tend to spin faster— men or women?

Typically, female skaters rotate faster—they can reach 246 RPMs on a triple spin. Male skaters spin a little slower, due to their greater body weight.

Spin Time

GET OUT YOUR MINUTE GLASS

This time trial is easiest on a stationary exercise bicycle, because most of them have an RPM (revolutions per minute) gauge, but you can also do it on a regular bicycle. (But no tricycles!)

Hop on your bicycle and set the gear resistance to low; you want to be able to pedal as fast as possible. **Can you match Lance Armstrong's 100 revolutions per minute?**

Pedal fast for 1 minute. If your bike has an RPM gauge, make sure you keep it at 100 RPMs for the entire minute. If not, count the number of times your right foot touches down.

Just imagine pedaling this fast for 23 whole days and over 2,000 miles like the Tour de France cyclists!

10

500
CD spins

A standard compact disc spins between 200 and 500 times every minute as it plays your favorite rock, pop, hip-hop, or other form of noise.

A regular CD holds 74 minutes of music. Why 74 minutes? In the early 1980s when Sony was developing this new technology, Sony's president, Norio Ohga, insisted that Beethoven's Ninth Symphony (which is almost exactly 74 minutes long) had to be able to fit on a single disc.

300,000
tooth-aching turns

The dizziest object on Earth is a dentist's drill.
It grinds at your tooth with 300,000 spins every minute.

Surely
you suspected that
that high-pitched squeal (the
drill's, not yours!) meant
serious business!

Hula Hullabaloo!

Remember when hula hoops® were the *coolest* toy on the block? No? Well, it *was* back in the 1950s. At the peak of their popularity, 144 hula hoops were sold every minute. Ask your grandparents.

The idea is, you swivel and twist your hips and get that hula hoop revolving around your waist. **Get out your minute glass and a hula hoop, and see how many complete hula hoop revolutions you can make in a minute** . . . that is, if you can keep it from falling down before the 60 seconds are up!

Tonya Lynn Mistal hula-hooped for 88 hours in a row (and the world record). That's over 3½ days of continuous hooping and a considerable amount of hullabaloo.

GET OUT YOUR MINUTE GLASS!

2½
windy miles

Hurricanes are enormous storms that form in the
ocean and sweep across the land. The most powerful
and destructive hurricanes are Category 5.
The winds swirl around at a speed of more than 2½ miles
per minute (156 miles per hour).

In 24 hours, a typical hurricane releases an incredible amount of total energy—
200 times the world-wide generating capacity. If only we could figure out
where to hook up the jumper cables!

5 ⅓
miles of twister

The fastest wind that's ever been recorded on Earth was in an Oklahoma tornado that traveled 5⅓ miles in a single minute (that's a speed of 320 miles per hour) in 1999.

What's even windier? The planet Neptune! The *Voyager 2* probe determined that Neptune's winds can blow at a speed of almost 25 miles per minute! A person would be literally blown away in such a wind. Yet another good reason to stay home on Earth.

CHAPTER 2

Peck, Punch, POW!

Knock, knock . . . anyone home? You'd never stand at a friend's house, knocking on the door at top speed for an *entire* minute, but if you did, you'd tap on the door around 300 times. (You'd also start to feel a little pain in your knuckles!) That motion—call it tapping, rapping, or pecking—takes place every minute in all sorts of ways . . .

15
slammin' punches

Boxer Philip Holiday landed a record 555 punches on his opponent during a championship fight. Ow! That's an average 15 punches every minute of all 12 rounds.

Plus, he threw lots more punches that didn't land.

Knockout!

Boxers in training spend hours hammering away at the speed bag to build up their speed and timing and more hours pounding on the heavy bag to build up their strength. **So how many punches can you throw in a minute, Rocky?**

A professional boxing bag and a pair of boxing gloves are the best things to use, but you can also practice hitting a thick stack of pillows or cushions propped against a wall. Flip your minute glass and fire away, counting how many times one hand connects with the padding.

Do be careful: Even though the pillows won't fight back, you can *really* hurt your hand if you accidentally hit the wall or anything else solid.

GET OUT **YOUR** MINUTE GLASS

19

100
pecks

Some species of woodpeckers can hammer their beaks against a tree 100 times in a minute. They do this to dig for insects, scoop out a comfy home for themselves, or to communicate with friends and relatives around the forest.

The palm cockatoo is an even more talented bird instrumentalist—it makes drumsticks from twigs and pounds them against a hollow log, accompanied by a charming twirling dance! MTV, are you listening?

133

push-ups

Jack Zatorski currently holds the push-ups record:

up, down, up, down . . . 133 times in a single minute. That's more than 2 push-ups every second!

Canadian Roy Berger did *only* 57 push-ups in a minute . . . but he kept it up for *an entire hour*, performing a total of 3,416 push-ups for another world record.

Push It!

I f you want to become a Navy SEAL, you must perform a minimum of 42 push-ups in 2 minutes. That's 21 push-ups per minute! Are you up to the challenge?

Hand your minute glass to someone else (you'll need both hands for the push-ups), and **see how many push-ups you can do in a minute**. You can try "modified push-ups," performed on your knees (they're easier), or fingertip push-ups, where your palms can't touch the floor (they're harder).

Push-ups build arm strength, and the stronger your arms, the more push-ups you'll be able to do in a minute. Leave the hour-long drill to the pros.

GET OUT YOUR MINUTE GLASS

900
pokes

A good sewing machine can jab its needle through a piece of fabric 900 times in a minute.

And a serious industrial sewing machine can make over 7,000 stitches per minute to stitch anything from your puffy winter coat to your favorite stuffed animal.

Keep your fingers out of the way!

23

1,200
blows

That noisy jackhammer banging away at the sidewalk
delivers around 1,200 blows in a minute.

While hardly as loud as a jackhammer (or as useful on a construction site),
when a cat purrs, it actually vibrates back and forth 1,560 times per minute!

6,000
rattles

When a rattlesnake feels threatened, the tip of its tail will buzz or rattle up to 6,000 times in a minute.

While baby humans love to play with rattles, a baby rattlesnake can't rattle at all! It has to shed several skins first.

Wagging

If you had a tail, you could calculate how many times it might wag in a minute. But you can measure how fast your dog's tail wags in a minute, unless it's one of those tailless breeds.

See if you can excite your dog with a treat, a trick, or a game to get that wagging up to maximum speed, then flip your minute glass and count. Cat owners can count their cat's tail swishes, but this may be trickier.

And why not see which dog is the waggingest in the neighborhood? Be sure and ask any dog's owner to help in the test; you don't want anyone wagging a finger at you.

GET OUT YOUR MINUTE GLASS

5,000
paint can shakes

Shake it up, baby! A paint shaker is a machine that shakes cans of paint back and forth really fast to mix up the paint—they're at your local paint store, shakin' their stuff 5,000 times in a minute (or more!).

If you're ever painting a wall or another big surface, your arm will make a back-and-forth motion too. If your hands are clean enough, you can use your minute glass to time your paint rate, but don't hurry, or paint will splash *everywhere*.

Possibly **one** earthquake

The planet Earth has a rhythm that's pretty regular too: earthquakes! And those loud, bumping beats occur about every 1½ minutes for a total of some 800,000 'quakes in a typical year. The Richter scale measures earthquakes on a scale of 1 (small) to 9 or more (catastrophic).

In the Netherlands, 1,000 citizens all jumped up and landed at the same time to see if they could register a little blip on the Richter scale. Sure enough, it registered as 1.2! If your school has close to that number of students, the thundering footsteps during the changing of classes might register a similar bump on the scale too.

CHAPTER 3

What's the Buzz?

The whining of a mosquito! The humming of a housefly! The droning of a bee! They're all the sounds of flapping wings, the same up-and-down or back-and-forth beat every minute . . .

300
butterfly flaps

The swallowtail butterfly is the slowest flapper of any flying insect. It flaps its wings 300 times in a minute—that's 5 flaps every second.

What the heck does *lepidopteran* mean? Lepidoptera is an order of insects with four broad wings that are often brightly colored—in other words, butterflies and moths!

31

Flappable You!

Maybe you think that the swallowtail butterfly is pretty pathetic, with only 300 flaps per minute! Well, let's see how many times you can flap your arms, smarty!

Turn over your minute glass, and count the number of times you can make long flaps with your arms (raising your arms over your head and then down to the sides of your body). Come anywhere near 300? Try again for another minute, holding your arms out to the side and just moving them up and down a few inches. Still nowhere near 300?

For your arms to create even the lowest hum or buzz, you'd have to move them as fast as 20 flaps per second! The more flaps per minute, the higher the sound you'll hear.

3,000
dragon-flaps

A dragonfly will flap its wings 3,000 times per minute.
This is fast enough for their wings to look like a blur.

People used to believe that dragonflies could sew your mouth shut!
In truth, dragonflies are pretty harmless, as well as just plain pretty.

4,800
flaps
(forward *or* backward)

Hummingbirds are the only birds that can maneuver
like tiny helicopters as they flap their wings up to
4,800 times per minute. They not only hover in midair and
feed from flowers, they can actually fly backwards!

The smallest hummingbirds
are about the size of a bee!
They flap their wings only
about 3,600 times per minute.

34

So just how fast do those mosquito wings beat? The new super "sonic" toothbrushes have cleaning bristles that stroke your teeth 31,000 times in a minute. Speaking of teeth, mosquitoes have 47 teeth, and not one has ever needed braces.

IN ONE PESKY MINUTE . . .

36,000
flaps . . . plus biting!

The annoying little mosquito flaps its wings 36,000 times every minute, creating that high-pitched whining noise.

12,000
wing-notes

A cricket isn't much of a flapper, but he's an amazing fiddler (yep, only the males make this noise). He scrapes the front part of one wing like a bow against the rough area of the other wing as if it were a violin.

A cricket varies its chirping speed according to the temperature: Hotter means chirpier. And certain crickets chirp 200 times per *second* when things really heat up.

A Cricket Thermometer

You don't need a thermometer to tell the temperature. You can use a snowy tree cricket! This cricket, which is found almost everywhere in the United States, gives a pretty accurate weather forecast in chirps.

Flip over your minute glass, and count the number of chirps it makes before the sand runs out. Now divide by 4.6, add 40, and there you have it: the temperature in degrees Fahrenheit.

Other crickets, some katydids, and some chirpy TV meteorologists also give the temperature, but you can't always be sure of their accuracy. And despite its name, you won't hear a weather report from the snowy cricket when it's cold enough to snow.

37

62,760
invisible flaps

A midge (also known as a no-see-um)
flaps 62,760 times in a minute. Midges are the fastest
flappers in the animal kingdom.

If you can't
see 'em, how do we know
how fast their wings
move?

Slowpokes Showdown

Throughout this multi-minute journey, a few races have been scheduled. Each race will last one minute, and they are a chance to compare the speeds of some noteworthy characters. And in this first competition are the ultimate slowpokes! At the end of a one-minute race, these contenders are pretty much right where they started. Some are tiny, some are enormous, but not one of them has any hustle . . .

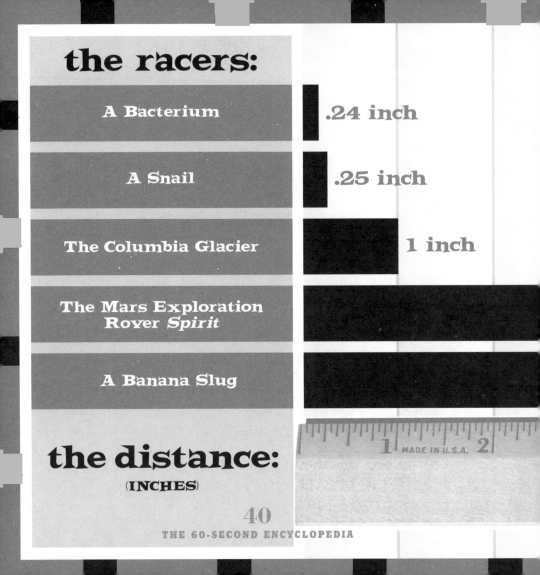

the racers:

A Bacterium — .24 inch

A Snail — .25 inch

The Columbia Glacier — 1 inch

The Mars Exploration Rover *Spirit*

A Banana Slug

the distance:
(INCHES)

1 MADE IN U.S.A. 2

40

SLOWPOKES SHOWDOWN

"Didn't they hear the starting gun? Oh wait, they *are* moving . . . but so slow that they're practically standing still. The glacier is barely gliding along, and the Mars Exploration Rover must be distracted with sightseeing. After 60 seconds of barely going anywhere, the banana slug is the fastest of the slowest."

5.7 inches

6.5 inches

A CLOSER LOOK AT OUR CONTESTANTS

THE WINNER!!

A Banana Slug!

Banana slugs are the second-largest slugs in the world, up to 10 inches long. They got their name because they look like black-spotted bananas!

2ND PLACE:

The Mars Exploration Rover *Spirit*

The *Spirit* doesn't travel all that fast, but it's tough when you're a solar-powered vehicle! Sure, Nascar isn't worried, but it's still the fastest vehicle on planet Mars.

3RD PLACE:

The Columbia Glacier

The Columbia Glacier is retreating, and its speed has actually increased! It travels away from Alaska's Prince William Sound at a rate of 115 feet per day.

4TH PLACE:

A Snail

Sure, most snails are slow, but there's one snail who's an athlete. In the World Snail Racing Championships, Archie sprinted more than 6 inches in 1 minute!

5TH PLACE:

A Bacterium

Don't badmouth bacteria! These tiny contenders travel 600 times their body length in a minute; a tuna, one of the fastest fish around, can swim only 60 times its body's length in a minute.

Last Place Bike Race!

In most races, you are supposed to go as fast as you possibly can. But sometimes it's even harder to go slow! Try this different kind of bicycle race.

You'll need your minute glass, a few friends, your bikes, and your bike helmets. Line up at the starting line, and have someone be the timekeeper. **Once the minute glass is flipped, the bikers try to go forward as little as possible,** pedaling only as much as necessary to keep balanced. At the end of a minute, the winner is the person in last place.

The only rules are: 1) If someone's foot touches the ground during the race, that person's out, and 2) No training wheels.

The Three-toed Sloth, at
8 feet

The three-toed sloth, found in tropical South and Central America, can travel only 6 to 8 feet per minute when ambling across the ground. But it can go twice as fast—about 15 feet per minute—when it's moving through the trees.

Sure, you could outrace a sloth any day, whether it's on the ground or in the trees. But the sloth would leave the rest of our "slowpokes" in its dust! It's just not fair to enter a sloth into the competition. Besides, the sloth needs its sleep—16 hours per day!

44

CHAPTER 4

Rock Around the Clock

Music and dancing go hand-in-hand (and foot-to-foot) because they're both all about the beat. Whether the slow, stately beat of a waltz or the fast pulse of a salsa, every minute 'round the clock is filled with rocking and rolling . . .

1,199
drumbeats

Jotan Afanodor, winner of "Battle of the Hands,"
is one of the world's fastest snare
drummers. His drumsticks can
hit the surface of a drum
1,199 times in 1 minute.

Tim Waterson on bass drums is winner of Extreme Sports Drumming's "Battle of the Feet." In 1 minute, using the foot pedals, he can stomp out 1,407 double strokes (alternately hitting a drum with two foot pedals).

IN ONE MINUTE OF TICKLING THE IVORIES . . .

3,000 piano notes

Liberace, the famously flamboyant (and fabulously wealthy) pianist, still holds the speed record for playing the most notes—3,000—in a single minute.

That's hitting an average of 50 keys each second (with only 10 fingers!) for a total of 60 seconds.

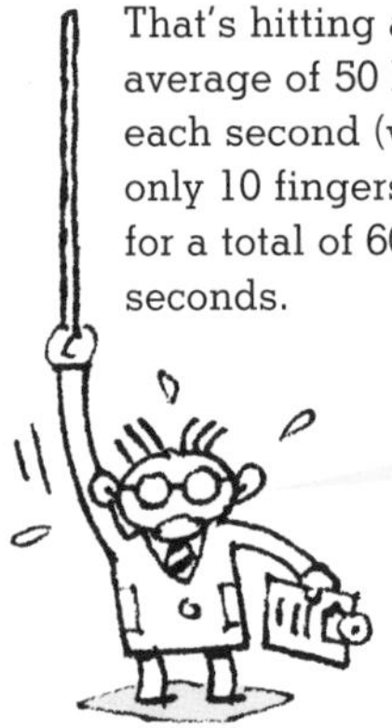

Makes you wonder how many words Liberace could type in a minute!

90
dancing steps

Let's add a dancer or two to the music! Waltzing
is one of the slowest ballroom dances, at a mere
90 steps per minute.

Other ballroom dances aren't much snappier either. The fox-trot is also 90 steps
per minute, and even a minute of the tango uses only about
96 barely-breaking-a-sweat steps.

49
THE 60-SECOND ENCYCLOPEDIA

128
do-si-dos

Square dancing requires an average 128 steps per minute
as you and your partner allemande, sashay, wheel around,
and promenade around the gymnasium. Yee-haw!

Another dance from elementary school is the bunny hop, which travels about
72 steps or hops per minute—and causes almost as much embarrassment.

134
boot scootin' steps

Square dancing too old-fashioned? Today's cowboys and cowgirls are busy country line dancing. Every minute of the "Boot Scootin' Boogie" takes 134 kicks, stomps, scoots, pivots, and swivels.

In January 2000, 6,275 people in Australia set the world record for the "Biggest Country Line Dance" by all performing the "Boot Scootin' Boogie." Talk about big boots to fill!

165
spicy steps

An exciting Latin dance like the salsa really starts to kick up the beat with as many as 165 steps every minute. *¡Olé!*

Extra spicy salsa with jalapeños is 50¢ extra.

200
speedy steps

So what's the fastest kind of ballroom dancing?
The Quickstep, which includes flips, skips, hips, dips
(and hopefully no slips), and other fancy footwork,
at 200 (or more!) steps per minute.

960

heel-stomping beats

Flamenco dancer Solero de Jerez, who was only 17 years old in 1967, could stomp his heels 16 times per second— that's 960 stomps in a minute.

Flamenco is a traditional Spanish dance that involves rapidly clapping your hands and stomping your heels on the dance floor. It's both a very athletic art and the perfect way to drive everyone in the room downstairs crazy.

54

Stomp!

How talented are you in the flamenco dance department? Can you come anywhere near Solero de Jerez's record?

Get out your minute glass and find a floor that can take some serious stomping! Forget your sneakers: Put on a pair of shoes that are going to make some noise!

Now, **count the number of times you stomp the heels of your shoes in one minute**. Remember, you're not simply running in place—you've got to make a nice stomping sound.

Did you come anywhere close to 1,000 stomps? How about 100?

1,440
taps

Ann Miller set an unofficial tap dance record in the 1944 movie *Hey Rookie* by tapping 500 steps in a minute. But in 1973, Roy Castle almost *tripled* Ms. Miller's record by tapping 1,440 steps in a minute—24 taps per second.

That's 2 feet making 24 sounds in a second.
Heck, most of us can barely put one foot in front of the other without tripping!

1,200
seats

When stadium sports fans "do the wave" at a big game,
the speed is nearly always 1,200 seats in a minute.

This also means
something like 2 dropped
hot dogs and 5 spilled
sodas every minute.

57

What Takes a Minute?

Lots of things *sound* like they take just a minute—but do they really? Does Minute® Rice take 1 minute to cook? Does "dinner will be ready in a minute" actually mean 60 seconds at your house? Does the Magic Minute Car Wash at the gas station only require 1 minute to soap, rinse, and dry your car?

Think of all those TV infomercials that claim it takes only 1 minute to "achieve rock-hard abs," "make money in your spare time," or "slice through an entire onion without shedding a tear." According to advertisements, you can accomplish most anything in a minute!

Maybe in some cases. But unfortunately, lots of people use the phrase "in just a minute" when they don't really mean it! Perhaps you should keep your minute glass handy for those occasions . . . to keep them honest!

On the other hand, think of all those dreadful jobs and chores that really would take "just a minute"—like taking out the trash or picking the laundry off the bedroom floor or even just apologizing to someone—that we spend hours or even days putting off!

Even if you have 1 miserable minute-long chore to do today, you've still got hundreds of minutes of fun left over. Assuming you need 480 minutes of sleep (8 hours) and 420 minutes of school (7 hours), that's still 539 happy minutes in your day. So go ahead and get that minute of pure drudgery over with!

CHAPTER 5

Jump to It!

Let's hop to it. Let's skip to it. Let's jump up and down and see what kind of ruckus we can make! Here's a jittery jumble of bouncing things that happen in a minute . . .

358
speed jumps

Veyom Bahl holds the American jump rope record:
358 jumps in a single minute.

The speediest jump ropers alternate feet, skipping over the rope with one foot
each time that the rope passes the ground.

Let's Go to the Hop

Grab your jump rope, because **it's time to see just how many times you can jump rope in a minute**. (Your minute glass should not jump with you; set it down or pass it to a friend.)

Are you faster hopping on both feet or skipping from one foot to the other as you jump rope? How fast can you go without getting all tangled up? And have you got a favorite jump rope rhyme?

Jumping rope is actually one of the best forms of exercise for your body. Check out pages 208–216 for more ways to burn a minutes worth of calories.

56
rump jumps

David Fisher holds the current record for rump jumping,
hopping over a turning rope from a sitting position.
He can sit on his bottom and bounce over a turning rope
56 times in 1 minute!

Some dogs enjoy jumping rope, too. A Russian wolfhound named Olive Oyl can skip rope 63 times in a minute. (There are also dogs who do not enjoy jumping rope; these include nearly all other dogs besides Olive Oyl.)

63
THE 60-SECOND ENCYCLOPEDIA

145
Pogo jumps

Boing, boing, boing . . . and 142 more *boings*.
Gary Stewart bounced on his Pogo Stick an average
145 times per minute for 20 hours and
20 minutes . . . and 177,737 jumps.

And if you'd prefer a unicycle over a Pogo Stick, you'll have to beat record holders
Constance Cotter and Peter Rosendahl who can each jump a unicycle over
a jump rope 169 times in a minute!

3,500
feet "down under"

The kangaroo bounds across the Australian outback, covering more than 3,500 feet in a minute. The 'roo's tail supports its body as it leans forward and pushes off into a jump that can be as high as 10 feet or as long as 30 feet.

The best human long jumpers in the world can barely leap 29 feet— and that's with a long, running start and a nice pit of sand to land in. And the best human high jumpers (not using a pole) leap about 8 feet up—high, but not 'roo high.

65

28
inches of spring-loaded sproing!

The tiny spittlebug could be the highest jumper in the animal kingdom. This garden pest can *sproing!* over 2 feet into the air without a running start or a vaulting pole. Sure, it doesn't jump a lot in a minute, but each hop is a doozy!

What, 2 feet and 4 inches doesn't seem very high? The spittlebug is the size of a pea, so it's jumping over 100 times its own height! In human-size terms, that's like a toddler jumping over the Statue of Liberty!

CHAPTER 6

Diggin' It

Instead of racing across land, these animals and machines dig into the dirt. They're the real earth-movers-and-shakers of the world. Just how "low" can they go in 60 seconds? Let's investigate—no, *let's excavate!*

5
inches

With armored bodies and long noses, armadillos look like
a cross between an anteater and a turtle. Built for digging,
they use their long, curved claws to dig small holes
to scavenge for worms and insects—they unearth
5 inches of dirt in a minute of diving for dinner.

An armadillo
can smell a worm
8 inches underground!

12

clammy inches

Clams often anchor themselves to a rock or a dock,
and call it a day. But clams can move! A Pacific razor clam
can dig through 9 to 12 inches of sand in a minute,
using its big foot. Even with a sand shovel,
you'd have a hard time outdigging an escaping clam.

18
subterranean inches

Moles can claw their way through 18 inches of mud in a minute. Busiest after dark, a single mole can dig a tunnel 300 feet long overnight.

Earthworms are a mole's favorite snack.

And a mole can outdig a wo

3
feet

The American badger is one of the best darn diggers in the animal kingdom—it can dig a hole faster than a man with a shovel! In soft soil, a badger can dig a hole and completely disappear from sight in one minute!

ndfolded . . . oh wait, it's already blind!

15
tons of coal

Coal-lossal! A continuous mining machine is lowered down a mine shaft to dig horizontally (not vertically), carving out a serious hole in the earth. The most powerful mining machines dig up 8 to 15 *tons* of coal in a minute.

Coal generates more than half of the electricity in the United States. And kids running across the carpet in their slippers may generate more than half of the *static* electricity in the United States.

How Fast Could You Dig to China?

Get out your timer, a ruler, and a shovel or trowel. Now dig for 1 minute, measure the hole's depth in inches, and then write down the number. Now go inside and grab a piece of paper and your calculator.

1. Multiply the number of inches you dug by 525,600 (the number of minutes in a year).

2. Now divide that figure by 63,360 (the number of inches in a mile).

3. Then divide 7,926 (the planet Earth's diameter in miles) by that number from step 2.

Ta-da! The answer you have is the number of years your dig will take you if you never sleep and/or slow down. And that's assuming you aren't roasted by Earth's 8,500°F molten core or crushed by the pressure (only about 900 times greater than on the surface).

19
salty tons

The salt mining machines on Louisiana's Avery Island
can mine 19 tons of salt in 1 minute.
That's enough salt to top 475 million pretzels.

Avery Island is the
same island where
the McIlhenny family
makes their famous
Tabasco sauce. (Above
ground, of course.)

CHAPTER 7

News Flash!

From lightning bolts to lightning bugs, every minute is illuminated with blinks, pulses, pops, and bursts of light that battle with the forces of darkness. Here's a news flash about some of the brightest lights around . . .

10
flying flashes

North America is home to 200 different species of fireflies, each with its own unique flash pattern. On a warm summer night, the males fly around and flash about 10 times in a minute (the females, down on the ground, reply approximately 2 seconds after each male's call).

Fireflies live in every state but California. (And why not? Well, they're pretty rare in most western states anyway. And Calfornia does have a few insects similar to fireflies. But nobody knows why fireflies just won't come to the Golden State.)

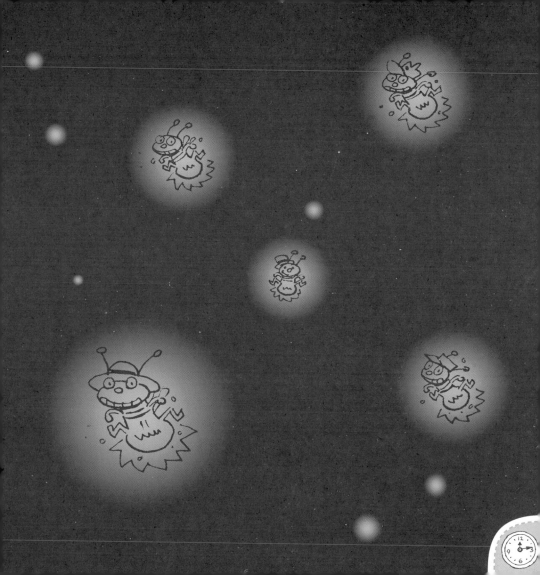

Don't Bug Me!

Fireflies, according to one ancient Japanese legend, are the souls of the dead. According to other legends, fireflies are just weird bugs with flashing bellies. But one thing is true: Every member of a particular species will flash the same number of times in a minute.

At dusk, gently nab a firefly in your hand or in a jar. If there's one perched on your screen door or a tree, you don't even need to catch him. **Invert your minute glass, and see how many times he flashes in a minute.** Chances are, if you catch any of his other flying buddies and count a minute of flashing, you'll get the same number.

On your next vacation, time the fireflies at the vacation spot and see if they're a different species from your hometown bugs.

28,824
snapshots

Every minute, 28,824 photographs are taken here in the United States. That's over 40 million per day! And at Walt Disney World, an estimated 822 pictures are taken every minute.

Your eyes blink an average of 15 times every minute. So there's a nearly 8% chance your eyes will be closed in a photograph. (And an even better chance that your eyes will look red or that you'll look goofy anyway.)

1,712
cars running red lights

Busted! Every minute, 1,712 cars and taxis run a red light in New York City. That's more than 1 million times every workday. And if a police officer happens to be nearby . . .

"Pull over, buddy!" The strobe lights on modern police cars can flash 70, 90, or 120 times in a minute.

1,200
fireworks explosions

A major big city's Fourth of July fireworks display shoots off up to 1,200 rockets every minute—about 36,000 during a 30-minute show. The "typical" fireworks spectacular costs $1,000 to $2,000 for each minute.

A box of sparklers, lit one a time, can last about half an hour, too, and that costs only a few bucks.

6,000
lighting bolts

Every minute, 6,000 lightning bolts illuminate Earth's skies somewhere. The good news is that 80% of all that stormy electrical activity is not cloud-to-ground lightning, but the in-cloud variety, that stays upstairs.

The typical bolt of lightning contains 30 million volts, heating the air around it to a toasty 50,000°F . . . hotter than the sun. (The voltage that powers all the outlets in your house is merely 110 volts.)

82

CHAPTER 8

Unidentified
Flying
Minutes

Objects in outer space burn, freeze, spin, and move
at amazing rates. The gravity of larger bodies
(like the sun or a planet) sets each object spinning
around like a top and traveling through space.
Even on planet Earth we're spinning around
every minute, even though
we can't feel it . . .

Topsy-Turvy

GET OUT YOUR MINUTE GLASS

The motion of planets spinning on their axes is much like a top spinning on a table. **Can you keep a top in motion for a whole minute?** Clear a space on a flat surface, invert your minute glass, and give the top a spin. (Gyroscopes work even better, if you have one.)

You'll notice that when the top is spinning fastest, it hardly appears to be moving at all. Because Earth moves at a fast, constant speed, you can't feel it spinning either. You'd only notice if it suddenly accelerated or slowed down.

But as the top's orbit tuckers out, it starts wobbling and moving in crazy circles. Don't worry—despite all those science-fiction disaster movies, Earth is not about to fly out of orbit.

17.4
miles traveled

If you stand on the equator, you'll move 17.4 miles every minute, even when you're standing still! That's because the planet Earth is whirling around in orbit and you're moving with it. Earth completes one rotation every 24 hours.

The sun you can see in the sky is really the sun from several minutes ago.
The actual sun has already moved—even at the speed of light, it still takes about
8 minutes and 18 seconds for a sunbeam to leap off the sun,
travel through outer space, and arrive in your backyard.

85
THE 60-SECOND ENCYCLOPEDIA

38⅓
moonlit miles

Our one and only moon scuttles along at 2,300 miles per hour (38⅓ miles each minute). In about 27 days, it makes a complete circle around Earth, which is how we got the whole idea of our monthly calendar in the first place.

So how far away is the moon? If you could somehow drive to the moon (imagine a lunar superhighway between your garage and the moon's parking lot!), it would take 181 days, driving 55 miles an hour and not stopping for gas or snacks or rest areas.

86
THE 60-SECOND ENCYCLOPEDIA

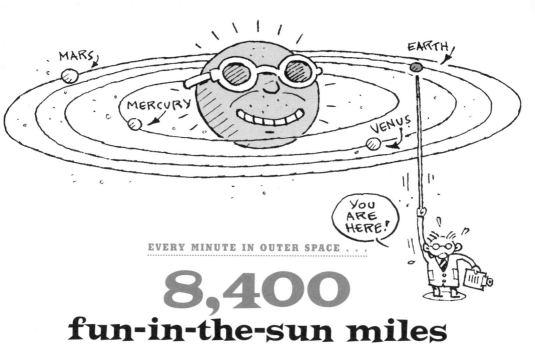

8,400
fun-in-the-sun miles

That bright yellow circle we call the sun gives us warm
days, healthy plants, and a good reason for sunscreen.
It travels 8,400 miles through space every minute, taking
all 9 planets of our solar system with it.

How old is the sun? Just over 4½ billion years old. Since no one's exactly sure
when its birthday is, don't feel bad about missing it every year.

87
THE 60-SECOND ENCYCLOPEDIA

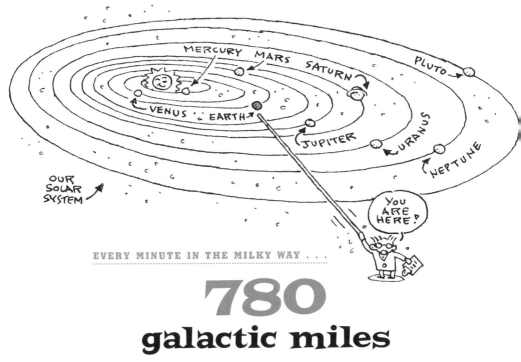

780
galactic miles

Our whole solar system is barreling through
its space neighborhood at the incredible speed
of 780 miles in a minute.

Some astronomers say the Milky Way galaxy has more than 200 billion stars, while
others think it's more like 400 billion stars. (Others say, "It's hard counting all those
little dots in the dark!")

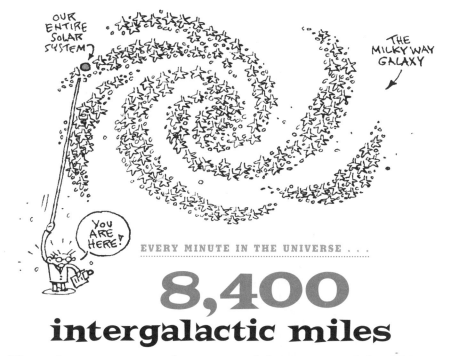

8,400
intergalactic miles

The solar system revolves around the center of the Milky Way galaxy at 8,400 miles per minute, and the Milky Way is also moving through space. You get the idea: Every single minute, everything in our universe is in motion.

Where the heck are we heading in such a hurry? Toward the Andromeda Galaxy. And in about 3 billion years, the two galaxies will collide. Abandon ship!

11,160,000
miles at the speed of light

Light from the sun, a star, a candle, a flashbulb,
or any other light source travels 186,000 miles
in a single second and 11,160,000 miles in a minute.

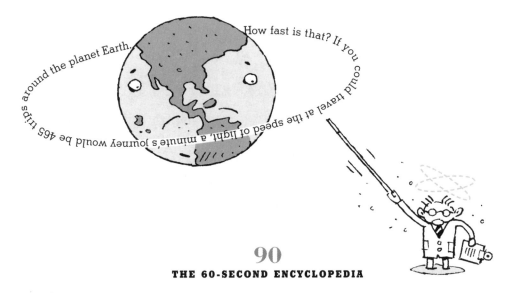

How fast is that? If you could travel at the speed of light, a minute's journey would be 465 trips around the planet Earth.

Seeing Stars

On a clear, starry night, count how many stars you can spot in a minute. Twenty? Forty? If there's no light pollution (meaning, streetlights and car lights and lights from storefronts), you should be able to see 3,000 stars! Stargazing is easier in the country, away from city lights.

You can't watch the stars spin on their axes, but you can see them rising and setting as the night goes on. And certain constellations appear and disappear with the changing seasons. A star guide will help you identify constellations like the Big Dipper, the North Star, and Orion. (A star map will help you track down your favorite celebrities in Hollywood.)

Want to see stars during the day? See how many times you can spin around in an entire minute!

83,714
noodle stars

The folks at Campbell's create 83,714 noodle stars every minute for their Chicken and Stars soup. That's over 44 billion noodle stars each year.

After years of making this soup, the Campbell's galaxy far outshines the real Milky Way!

PART 2

Time Is Money!

Buying and spending, selling and lending, every minute is filled with money, whether you're earning it or shelling it out.

Shopping Spree

Thankfully, everyone in the United States doesn't go shopping at the same time. (Just imagine what the checkout lines would be like!) But collectively we do spend a lot of time shopping. Here's a sample of some of our purchasing power. In 1 minute, our shop-till-you-drop nation buys . . .

4
Barbie® dolls

Barbie is an all-American doll, but she now "lives" in over 140 countries around the world where a total of 120 Barbies are purchased every minute.

Barbie was born "Barbie Millicent Roberts" in 1959. This makes her not only the most popular, but also the best-preserved, 46-year-old in the world.

8,333
crayons

Crayola® sells an average 8,333 crayons every minute.
That's nearly 3 billion crayons per year—and millions
of crayon art masterpieces hung on bulletin boards.

Kids spend an average 28 minutes every day coloring. If you add up all those kids in the U.S., that's 6.3 billion hours of coloring every year.

455
video games

That's 355 console games, plus another 100 computer games, sold every minute. Imagine having the time and money to actually play (and win!) all those games.

What's the best-selling video game of all time? It's a classic: Super Mario Bros., with 40 million total units sold. If Mario and Luigi were real, they'd be billionaires!

8

Tonka® trucks

The first Tonka truck was made in 1947, and these tough toys were so popular that the entire inventory sold out in just a few months. More than 250 million Tonka trucks have been sold since then, averaging more than 8 trucks every minute.

Every year, Tonka uses more than 119,000 pounds of yellow paint and 5.1 million pounds of sheet metal to make its trucks and construction vehicles.

312
packages shipped

Some folks like shopping from the comfort of the TV room.
Roughly 312 packages are shipped every minute from
the two biggest television shopping networks, Home
Shopping Network and QVC. Operators are standing by!

$1,902,588
charged on Visa® cards

More than $1 trillion is charged on Visa cards every year in the United States. Sure, there are other credit cards, such as American Express, MasterCard, and Discover, but all those cards' purchases combined don't equal the amount charged on Visa cards.

There are 429 million Visa cards held in the United States, and, between Thanksgiving and Christmas, over $2 million is charged every minute.

Supermarket Challenge!

Take a look at the cans, boxes, cartons and jars in a supermarket—they're all competing for your attention. "New and Improved!" "World Famous!" "Delicious!" (How can they all be "The Best"?!!) **How many examples of this advertising frenzy can you find in a minute?**

Start by choosing just one word or phrase, such as *"New," "Best," "Famous,"* or *"Greatest."* Position yourself at the head of an aisle that's full of products and packages, like cereals, snacks, or cleaning products.

Flip over your timer and go! You get 1 point each time you find your word or phrase on a product, plus a bonus point if there's an exclamation point! Like this! Super job!

cars

Every minute, dealerships across the U.S. sell 32 cars and light trucks. Of course, that's nothing compared to the 120 Hot Wheels® cars sold around the world each minute.

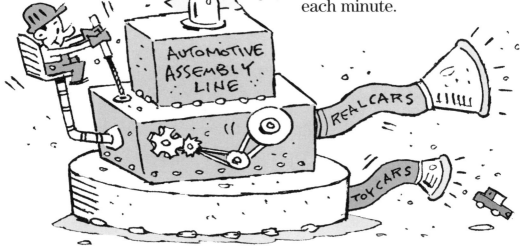

Some motorists think two wheels are better than four! One Harley-Davidson motorcycle enters the world every 1 minute and 45 seconds (that's about 300,000 "Hogs" every year).

103
THE 60-SECOND ENCYCLOPEDIA

190
houses built

Parker Brothers builds 100 million houses every year for Monopoly, the best-selling board game in the world. That's 190 new homes every minute . . . and that's not counting all the hotels! Too bad you can't move in.

How do they pay for all that construction? They have their own mint! Every minute they print $95,129 in Monopoly money, for a total of $50 billion each year.

Horse Power
vs.
Horsepower

For thousands of years, horses were the #1 form of transportation for people all around the globe. Horses carried us into battles, across empty deserts, and through endless wilderness. But then, 100 years ago, the automobile came along, and put most horses out to pasture, so to speak. So how does a pretty pony compare to a pretty Porsche?

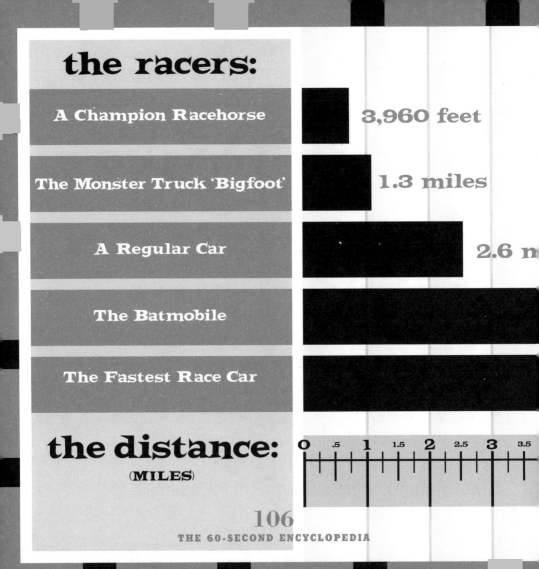

the racers:

A Champion Racehorse — 3,960 feet

The Monster Truck 'Bigfoot' — 1.3 miles

A Regular Car — 2.6 m

The Batmobile

The Fastest Race Car

the distance:
(MILES)

0   .5   1   1.5   2   2.5   3   3.5

ONE-MINUTE RACE
HORSE POWER vs.
HORSEPOWER

"The racehorse was off to a flying start! But so was the competition, and those vehicles left him in their dust—they're all definitely breaking the speed limit. After 60 seconds of putting the pedal to the metal, the racecar is the winner by a long shot."

5.8 miles

12.7 miles

5   5.5   **6**   6.5   **7**   7.5   **8**   8.5   **9**   9.5   **10**   10.5   **11**   11.5   **12**   12.5   **13**

A CLOSER LOOK AT OUR CONTESTANTS

THE WINNER!!

The Fastest Race Car!

Andy Green's racing speed of 763 miles per hour was supersonic—literally! It was the first time a land vehicle had ever broken the sound barrier.

2ND PLACE

The Batmobile

The newest Batmobile can really fly, but the original Batmobile from the 1966 TV series wasn't half as fast, because it was just a regular car. It was a 1955 Lincoln Futura painted shiny black with big bat-fins.

3RD PLACE:

A Regular Car

On Germany's Autobahn motorway, there are no posted speed limits, so you can take your car to its absolute top speed without worrying about getting a speeding ticket.

4TH PLACE:

The Monster Truck 'Bigfoot'

Bigfoot isn't the fastest, even with its gigantic tires, but it's quite a jumper. In 1999, Bigfoot #14 (there's more than one of them) leapt 202 feet over a 727 jetliner.

5TH PLACE

A Racehorse

Horse racing is still popular today, and racehorses really do move fast, even if cars are faster. In 1 minute, horses are about halfway around the Kentucky Derby racetrack.

Sweep-Skates!

Before you even read this paragraph, go put on your helmet, gloves, kneepads, and elbow pads. . . . All right, you ready now? The challenge is: **How many feet can you travel in a minute on your skateboard?** You'll need to be at a skateboard park, empty parking lot, or other cleared paved space.

Have a buddy hold the minute glass, take off when he yells "Go!," and then come to a stop as soon as you hear the minute's up. Pace off the distance with your feet, a tape measure, or retrace your course with the odometer on your bike. You'll have your skateboarding speed either in feet or miles per minute.

Of course, you can also measure your speed on roller skates, in-line skates, or scooters . . . but do be careful. Speed's no fun if you get hurt.

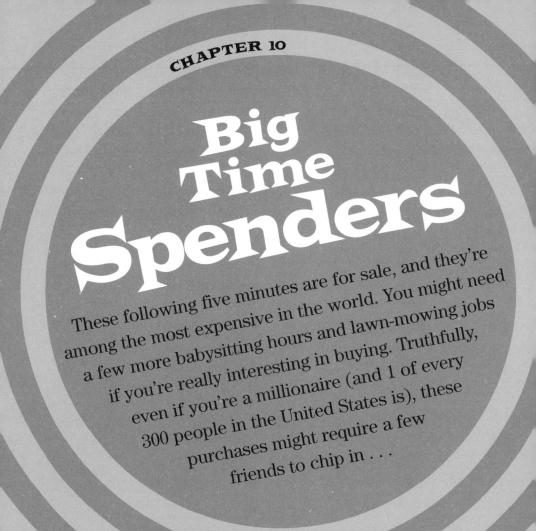

CHAPTER 10

Big Time Spenders

These following five minutes are for sale, and they're among the most expensive in the world. You might need a few more babysitting hours and lawn-mowing jobs if you're really interesting in buying. Truthfully, even if you're a millionaire (and 1 of every 300 people in the United States is), these purchases might require a few friends to chip in . . .

$4,200,000
for a Super Bowl commercial

Want to buy yourself a minute-long commercial during the Super Bowl? It will set you back $4.2 million (or over $70,000 for each second).

The good news? Over 130 million people will be watching. Some folks think the commercials are even better than the game! Or the snacks!

$1,736
for each minute in space

Jedi, robot companions, and light sabers each sold separately.

Yes, for a mere $20 million, you, too, can spend 8 days in space. The first space tourist to finance his own flight aboard a Russian space mission was millionaire Dennis Tito. He circled Earth 128 times and expressed his hopes that, one day, all people will enjoy such space travels.

$68,181
for a TV cartoon minute

That's the cost of creating just 1 minute of *The Simpsons*, or another top-quality animated TV series. Every minute requires 1,440 images to be drawn, colored, and animated— and there are whole teams of writers, producers, actors, and receptionists that have to be paid as well.

Dino-soaring costs! The TV documentary *Walking with Dinosaurs* used computer animation, and it cost $61,112 to create each minute, for a total of nearly $10 million.

$3,805,175
for a minute of government spending

The United States of America's biggest spender is . . . the United States. The U.S. government spends close to $2 trillion per year, or $3,805,175 each minute, on public education, national parks, defense, and thousands more programs.

Where does all this cash come from? Taxes, fines, tolls . . . so that (hopefully) the government earns more than it spends.

$1,704,545
for a minute of movie-making history

The animated feature *Tarzan* holds the record for the most expensive movie minutes in history: Each minute cost over $1.7 million to create, at a mere 88 minutes and a total budget of $150 million.

As of *this* minute, *Harry Potter and the Goblet of Fire* has the largest film budget ever—$305 million. But if it runs over 2½ hours, it won't beat *Tarzan's* money-per-minute record.

15,838
coins

Whether your spare change comes from an allowance, a job, or your savings account, the actual nickels and dimes are minted by the United States Mint. It produces 15,838 coins each minute. (Bills are printed elsewhere.)

In 1 minute, it mints 11 golden dollars, 12 half-dollars, 2,822 quarters, 2,859 dimes, 1,852 nickels, and 8,285 pennies.

it costs just over a dime to make a golden dollar

it costs just less than a dime to make a half-dollar

it costs almost a nickel to make a quarter

it costs nearly 2 pennies to make a dime

it costs over 3 pennies to make a nickel

it costs almost a penny (.81¢) to make a penny

Does that even make sense— or cents?

Model Minutes

Speaking of the government, some minutes are more official
than others. They may not be covered by national laws,
but some minutes must abide by official rules, directions, scientific
principles, or common sense. Here are some examples of these stricter
minutes. Think of others and add them to this list.

It takes a minute for...

- a full time-out at a basketball game

- military troops to march exactly 90 steps, each 28 inches in length
  (that's the definition of what the military calls "common time")

- the rest period between rounds
  in a boxing match

- your microwave to heat up one
  breakfast Hot Pocket®

- a professional actor or singer to
  audition for a casting director

- a standard thermometer to read your temperature accurately

- boiling water to remove any harmful bacteria or parasites

- a player to make one move in a game of Pictionary® or Password™

- a speech on any topic that any member of Congress may deliver before or after the big legislative business of the day

- the elevator ride to the top of the Empire State Building where you get a King Kong perspective of New York City from the 86th-floor observatory

- a proper hand-washing session so your hands are clean enough to pass inspection from Mom!

- a competitive weightlifter to press or lift the weight once he or she announces "ready"

CHAPTER 11

Made in the United States

In factories, bakeries, and plants, American businesses are busy producing things to sell. Here's a sample to whet your wallet (and your appetite) . . .

10
fortune cookies

Employees at the Fortune Cookie Factory in
Oakland, California, can hand-fold fortunes
into 10 fortune cookies
each minute.

Think fortune cookies came from China? Think
again! They were invented in San Francisco.

208
cans of Play-doh®

The Play-doh factory at Hasbro produces
208 six-ounce cans of their own 'doh each minute.

Although a day's
worth of Play-doh
(300,000 cans) might
smell good enough to
eat, you should *only*
make pretend noodles
from this 'doh.

245
pretzels

On a state-of-the-art pretzel-twisting machine,
245 pretzels can be made each minute. Isn't it nice
to know that even the humble pretzel has a
"state of the art"?

Pretzels have been a favorite snack for hundreds of years—
it's even rumored that the Pilgrims twisted pretzels on Plymouth Rock
(though not literally on the Rock itself!).

GET OUT YOUR MINUTE GLASS

Twist and Shout

Today's human pretzel-twisters shape about 57 pretzels in a minute. What's your twist-ability?

Open a refrigerated package of pretzel dough or breadstick dough and separate the dough into individual sticks. Then, using the diagram below, **see if you can twist all 12 pretzels in a minute's time**.

Once you've finished, brush the tops of the pretzels with lightly beaten egg, dust with kosher salt, and bake according to package directions with an adult's supervision.

If you don't have a package of dough handy, you can use Play-doh, modeling clay, even pipe cleaners. Just don't put them in the oven or snack on them!

867
Twinkies®

Meanwhile, at just one Twinkie bakery, 867 delicious little
sponge cakes can be filled with cream in a single minute.

Hostess bakes 500 million Twinkies every year. That takes 8 million
pounds of sugar and 40,000 miles of cellophane wrapping!

4,000
cans of soda pop

Whether you call it pop, soda, or just "that fizzy stuff,"
a single plant can fill 4,000 cans with a carbonated beverage
in a single minute.

22,831
Oreos®

All those minutes of Oreo-eating add up to 12 billion
Oreos sold in just one year. Oreo is the #1 selling cookie
in the world, and some 450 billion of these cream-filled
favorites have been bitten, unscrewed, nibbled,
and dunked since its 1912 debut.

Regular Oreos too "healthy" for you? Many fairs have started selling battered and
deep-fried Oreos. Many fair-goers ought to have their heads examined!

5,556
lollipops

Meanwhile, 5,556 Dum Dum® lollipops pop out of the machines at the Spangler candy factory in Bryan, Ohio, every minute—that's 8 million suckers a day.

Apparently, the saying "A sucker is born every minute" ought to be "5,556 suckers are born every minute."

5,000
animal crackers

The Nabisco factory produces an estimated
5,000 animal crackers every minute. That's 15,000 boxes
every hour, enough to feed a zoo!

The string handle on the box of Barnum's animal crackers was originally added so
the boxes could be hung from Christmas trees.

55,555
Hershey's Kisses®

Hershey's chocolate factories in California and Hershey, Pennsylvania, make an average of 55,555 Kisses each minute, for a total of 80,000,000 each day.

How many Kisses equal a pound of chocolate?

look for the answer on the next page...

A BIG KISS

277,778
M&Ms®

Red, green, blue, or brown—no matter the color, 277,778 M&Ms are made every minute, meaning that more than 400 million of these tiny treats are dipped and coated every day.

Mmmmm . . . the average American eats 12 pounds of chocolate each year.

CHAPTER 12

Nursery Times

Every minute of every day, puppies, kittens, and babies are born, rather than manufactured (you knew that). Of course, all these newborns *do* provide manufacturers with reasons to make smooshed-up peas and baby powder and fluffy things that go *squeak-a, squeak-a . . .*

7²/₃
babies are born

Though the number of births changes a little every year, nearly 8 babies are born every minute in the United States. That's a total of more than 4 million new reasons to worry about sharp corners each year.

The average person—that's you—shares a birthday (same day, same year) with about 11,000 other people in the United States. And you share your birth *minute* with about 8 of those people.

it's twins!

More and more women are having multiple births: A set of twins is now born once every 4 minutes.

A group of triplets, quadruplets, quintuplets, or even more, are born about every 72 minutes.

49
puppies and kittens are born

Nearly seven times more kittens and puppies are born in the United States than babies every minute. And that's just an estimate, because it's impossible to keep track of all the stray dogs and cats that are in need of loving families.

Even if everyone in the United States adopted a puppy or kitten, there will still be millions of animals who won't ever find homes. Spaying and neutering helps to limit the number of unwanted cats and dogs (and that's one thing your family can do this minute to help).

34,200
new diapers

Every minute, 34,200 babies are changed in the United States, meaning we need 34,200 fresh diapers. (A typical baby will go through as many as 10,000 diaper changes.)

At the same time, an estimated 7,610 pounds of kitty litter are thrown out every minute because no one's come up with kitty diapers.

Oh, but someone has! It's just that no one wants to change them!

Trash Day

Hold your nose, this is going to get a little stinky. Here's what we (more than 290 million Americans) throw away in a single minute, all day long, all year long. Just be glad you're not the only one in charge of taking out the trash . . .

41,667
plastic bottles

Milk bottles, water bottles, soda bottles—
41,667 plastic bottles are thrown away every minute.
And only a small fraction get recycled.

Crash! We also toss out 24 tons of glass every minute,
including jars and bottles that could be recycled.

14
Beetles, Falcons, Mustangs, Rabbits . . .

No, silly, not animals—cars!
Fourteen cars are heaped into junk piles each minute.
These include crashed cars, trash-compacted cars,
cars dismantled for parts, and other vehicles
that can't be driven again.

In that same minute, we toss out 2 or 3 trucks and buses, 514 tires, and 5,137 batteries. (Ninety-seven percent of lead-acid batteries— the kind used in cars, trucks, and boats—are recycled.)

99,696
pounds of food

This isn't just the sour milk or soggy salad in our refrigerators, but also food from restaurants, grocery stores, and hotels that can't be saved.

It sounds like a huge waste, but regulations require restaurants and stores to offer only the safest, freshest food.

Many organizations work to quickly transport perishable foods to food pantries and shelters where they can provide a "second helping" for families at risk of hunger.

127,854
pounds of trash

In addition to all of the trash that gets thrown into dumps and landfills, 150,325 pounds of trash are burned across the United States every minute.

Taking out the trash is an annoying chore, but informal polls
say that cleaning the bathroom and washing dishes are considered much worse!

53

tons of leaves and grass

Across our 50 states, the seemingly innocent bags of grass clippings, leaves, and other yard trimmings set out by the curb mount up. They compose 53 tons (over 106,500 pounds) each minute, and that adds up to 28 million tons in a whole year.

There are more than 3,000 waste composting programs that are helping people "turn over a new leaf" when it comes to yard waste.

Yes, You Can Can!

Every minute, Americans recycle 119,102 aluminum cans. **So how many cans can you personally recycle in a minute**? You'll need a few dozen empty aluminum cans, a big plastic bag, and good can-stomping shoes. Now place the cans, right side up, in a long line along the sidewalk or driveway.

Flip over the timer, and stomp each can until it is flat. Quickly stuff the compacted can into your recycling sack, and go on to the next can, trying to crush as many cans as you can in a minute. *Take that, Mountain Dew! In your face, Dr Pepper!*

Now, no one expects you to *completely* recycle a can (unless you have a metal foundry in your backyard) so the last step is to pitch your flattened cans into the nearest recycling bin.

122
tons of garbage

In the past decade, our nation's recycling efforts have grown more than 16%; now almost 30% of materials that can be recycled actually are. That means that every minute, 122 tons of materials like aluminum, paper, glass, and plastic are recycled instead of just thrown away.

So what *can* you just toss in the trash? Well, fish bones, Q-tips, and empty tubes of toothpaste.

PART 3

It's Feeding Time!

Steak, ice cream, hot dogs, even insects—every minute, millions of creatures are munching a meal.

CHAPTER 14

Mealtime Minutes

Even the hungriest animals don't eat all 1,440 minutes in a day. Some animals devour their food in one sitting or eat only once a week while others nibble for hours. That means some creatures eat a lot in a minute while others take only a bite or two. Wander into the wild world and witness some of the munching and crunching that goes on every minute . . .

150
flicks of the tongue

An anteater wanders around, snacking on as many as 30,000 ants and other insects every day. Its quickly flicking, sticky tongue flips in and out 150 times per minute, scooping up hundreds of ants in 60 seconds.

Anteaters are very, very happy campers because there are more ants than any other living thing in the world: an estimated 1 quadrillion ants at any one time.

147
THE 60-SECOND ENCYCLOPEDIA

GET OUT
YOUR
MINUTE
GLASS
!

Lickety-Split

Humans are lucky enough to have hands and teeth, as well as forks and knives, to help us eat our food. But what if you only had your tongue to help you eat? Could you eat as well as an anteater?

Take a plate and sprinkle it with a thin layer of shelled sunflower seeds, loose granola, crumbled-up crackers, or any other snack that is small and light.

Flip over your minute glass, and see how much you can eat in a minute using just your tongue to bring the food into your mouth. The bits should stick to your tongue, just like ants stick to the tongue of an anteater! (Yes, you can also use ants if you really want an accurate comparison.) You probably won't flick your tongue 150 times, but can you clean your plate?

10
mosquitoes

A little brown bat nabs up to 10 mosquitoes in a minute,
and it'll eat up to 3,000 mosquitoes in a single night.

There are nearly 1,000 different bat species,
nearly a quarter of all mammal species on Earth. That's a battalion of bats!

1

big, lip-smacking, tusk-tempting mouthful of clams

A walrus dives in the ocean, swims to the bottom, and uses its mouth like a vacuum cleaner to suck clams right out of the sand! It snacks on about 4,000 clams in one long feeding.

Shucks! Clams don't come preshucked, so the walrus spends much of his mealtime prying open clams and spitting out shells.

2
bamboo shoots

A giant panda chomps about 2 shoots of bamboo every minute during its daily 12-hour meal. Pandas eat around 40% of their body weight each day, up to 80 pounds of food, depending on how *giant* each panda actually is.

You might feel especially motivated by pizza day at the cafeteria, but you should stop long before you get to 40% of your body weight.

1
salmon snack

A grizzly bear grabs a whole salmon out of a river using just its paw! Some bears eat the whole fish, but picky grizzlies just take a bite or two before dropping the salmon and going to catch a new one. Grizzlies eat up to 90 pounds of salmon in one day.

Grizzlies eat over 20,000 calories every day when preparing for hibernation. That's the caloric equivalent of eating 33 Big Macs every day (although bears rarely have a chance to order burgers—or even Filet o' Fish sandwiches).

Chowing Down

Does your pet dog or cat eat daintily, or does it "wolf down" its food? Here's how to measure its chow-down time.

First, measure the kibble or canned food you feed your pet using measuring cups and tablespoons, and write the amount down.

Call your pet for supper, **place the bowl down in its usual place, and flip over your timer.** When the minute glass is empty, retrieve the bowl, quickly measure the remaining food, and then let your pet finish supper. Subtract the amount of remaining food from the amount of total food placed in the bowl and you'll have your pet's rate of eating per minute.

*If you have a dog who has shown any aggressive behavior at all regarding food or toys, don't disturb its dinner. Instead, divide its total dinner amount by the total number of minutes it takes to finish.

GET OUT YOUR MINUTE GLASS

153

THE 60-SECOND ENCYCLOPEDIA

5½
pounds of krill

A blue whale will eat 5½ pounds of krill in a minute,
for a total take-out meal of 8,000 pounds every 24 hours.

Krill are tiny
crustaceans, like
crayfish or shrimp.
Each female krill
can lay 10,000
eggs at one time,
so millions of blue
whale dinners are
always being
prepared.

155
THE 60-SECOND ENCYCLOPEDIA

71

cud chews

A cow spends more than 14 hours every day chewing! Cows chow down on about 40 pounds of grass or feed every day, and they munch their food at a rate of 71 chews per minute.

Cows also spend hours rechewing their own partially digested food, known as *cud*. The next time someone reminds you to thoroughly chew your food before you swallow, just be glad you're not a cow.

Double (Bubble) Time

Just as cows chew cud, people chew gum! Hundreds of years ago, people used to cut pieces of tasty spruce sap to chew on. It inspired inventors to create something a little better than that, resulting in the minty fresh and sugary pink stuff we chew today.

Do you chew your gum fast or slow? **Pop in a piece of gum, flip your minute glass, and count the number of chews you take.** Slow: 50 chews or less; Medium: 51–110 chews; Fast: 111 or more.

Now for a bubble-blowing challenge. Can you unwrap a piece of bubble gum, pop it in your mouth, and blow a bubble . . . all in under a minute?

1

nice side salad

Speaking of cows, a manatee, also known as
a sea cow, enjoys 2 ounces of salad (plants and grasses)
every minute, 6–8 hours of the day.

All manatees are vegetarians. Wild manatees eat sea grasses, but in
captivity, they're often fed romaine and iceberg lettuce:
over 200 heads each day. A manatee can live to the age of 70 . . . that's a lifetime
total of 5 million heads of lettuce without a single drop of ranch dressing!

8
ounces of "trail mix"

An African elephant spends about 16 hours every day crunching its own version of "trail mix": nearly 8 ounces of twigs, grass, fruit, and other vegetation every minute. That's the weight of half a box of breakfast cereal, although you won't find *that* in the African bush.

Elephants spend so much time eating, yet they digest only about 40% of the food they consume.

Hmm, why am I still hungry?

159
THE 60-SECOND ENCYCLOPEDIA

drops of blood

A leech drinks about 6 drops of blood each minute.
It slurps up to 1 tablespoon of blood in about 30 minutes,
10 times its normal body weight.

Vampire bats will drink 2 or more tablespoons of blood during a feeding.
They prey on sleeping cows and other mammals, but when a bat can't find food,
its bat friends will share a little regurgitated blood.

3
pounds of the finest wildebeest

A lion and a lioness can eat 15 and 11 pounds of food a day, respectively. But these big cats usually eat one huge, quick meal of zebra, wildebeest, or another meat—a feast that lasts only a few minutes.

A wild lion can eat as much as 80 pounds of meat in one feeding! A meal that size will fuel its body for several days, until it catches another dinner.

1/4
of a berry

Or a nibble of nut, plus the odd bug or two

The short-tailed shrew is a tiny critter, only weighing 1 oz., but it's got a mean appetite. The most voracious animal in the whole animal kingdom, it eats as much as 3 times its body weight in food every day!

Can you
imagine eating
3 times your own
body weight?!!

The Animal Olympics

Now presenting . . . the Animal Kingdom Olympics, a 60-second race across the land. Now, this race wouldn't really take place for several reasons, including:

1) Many of the contestants live on different continents and don't travel

2) Some contestants would rather eat the competition for lunch

3) One contestant is extinct!

the racers:

A Black Mamba Snake & A Squirrel
1,056 feet

Tyrannosaurus Rex & A Wild Turkey
1,320 feet

A Grizzly Bear, A House Cat, & A Giraffe
.5 mile

A Rabbit & A Zebra
.58 mi

A Cheetah

the distance:
(MILES)

0   .25   .5

ONE-MINUTE RACE
THE
ANIMAL
OLYMPICS

"There they go! Looks like size really doesn't matter . . . the T. Rex and the grizzly bear are losing to the rabbit. The zebra and giraffe are kicking up dust, and with their striped and spotted uniforms, they look cool too. The house cat is fast, but it's the kitty's cousin, the cheetah, who's top cat after 60 seconds."

1.6 miles

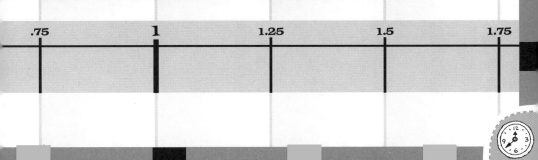

.75   1   1.25   1.5   1.75

A CLOSER LOOK AT OUR CONTESTANTS

THE WINNER!!

A Cheetah!

Cheetahs are the fastest cats on the planet.
And they're also the only cats that always have their
claws extended. In fact, their paws look a lot like a dog's paws.

2ND PLACE:
A Rabbit & A Zebra

Rabbits are fast runners, and they also make excellent pets. Not zebras—they're from the same family as horses, but they cannot be tamed and ridden. (Too bad—imagine the Lone Ranger riding a zebra!)

3RD PLACE:
A Grizzly Bear, A House Cat, & A Giraffe

Grizzlies are fond of long winter naps, and cats also love to doze. But the giraffe sleeps standing up, and rarely snoozes for more than 20 total minutes per day.

4TH PLACE:
A T. Rex & A Wild Turkey

These two run at the same speed, but a wild turkey can actually fly much faster— 55 mph. Domestic turkeys (the kind you eat) are too heavy to fly more than a few feet.

5TH PLACE:
A Black Mamba & A Squirrel

The black mamba is proud to be the fastest, most aggressive venomous snake in the world. The squirrel, however, is content to nibble nuts, climb trees, and look cute.

9
quarts of air

You take about 15 full breaths and inhale 9 quarts of air every minute . . . and that's when you're at rest. Lungs on the run require lots more air.

Picture 2 empty plastic milk gallon jugs and one empty quart—that's about how much air your lungs take in (and push out) in a minute.

Hold It!

The average person breathes 15 times in a minute. But you can also exert some control over your breathing: choosing how deeply to inhale or how long to hold each breath. Can you hold your breath for one entire minute?

Take a nice deep breath, so that you fill your lungs, and . . . hold! Turn over the timer, and be calm. **See if you can hold your breath until all the sand has fallen into the other half.** (Hint: Try not to laugh.)

Exercise, as well as breathing practice, will increase your lungs' capacity. People who practice yoga or other breathing techniques take very few breaths per minute and hold the air in their lungs much longer. Harry Houdini, the famous magician, claimed he could hold his breath for hours!

GET OUT YOUR MINUTE GLASS

1

taste bud bites the dust

The pattern of your tongue's 10,000 taste buds is as unique as your fingerprints. Each of those taste buds lasts only about a week or two before it is worn out and a new taste bud takes its place.

With all the eating, drinking, and talking it does every day, your tongue gets a serious workout. It's even brawny enough to bench press a bagel!

1²/₃
miles of speedy sneezing

A sneeze bursts forth from your nose with a force greater than some hurricanes. It explodes out at a speed of 1⅔ miles in a minute—over 100 miles in an hour! A cough blasts forth from your mouth with the velocity of a "whole gale": It travels 1 mile per minute, or 60 miles per hour.

THE 60-SECOND ENCYCLOPEDIA

.0000028
inches of nail power

Fingernails and toenails are really slow growers:
Each one takes about 6 months to grow from the base
to the tip. That's about ⅛ of an inch every month,
or .0000028 inches each minute.

Nails are actually made of the same material as your hair—
a protein called keratin. They're just a little denser, harder, and better suited
for jobs like scratching or wearing glittery polish.

HMMM...

40,000
skin cells are shed

You shed your entire "hide" every 27 days or so,
which means you'll have worn 1,000 new skins
by the time you're 80 years old.

> Gimme some skin!
> All those skin cells your
> body sheds add up to about
> 1 1/2 pounds total in
> a year!

96
dripping drops of sweat

Your body sweats to keep cool, and when it's hot or
you're really working hard, you can lose as much as
96 drops per minute, or 3 gallons a day. Sounds like a lot?
Each square inch of your skin contains 650 sweat glands.

A pair of feet can contribute as much as 1 cup of sweat each day.

5
quarts of blood

While you're relaxed or asleep, your heart pumps over
5 quarts of blood in a minute. Once you start exercising,
your heart starts pumping more than 5 *gallons* of blood
in a minute—4 times as much.

Amazing?
Sure, but not as
amazing as a giraffe's
heart, which pumps 16
gallons of blood up and
down that long neck
every minute!

2

ounces of perfectly natural gas

Most people expel about 32 ounces of gas every day,
for an average of ¹⁄₅₀ ounce per minute. In 1 minute,
in a crowded school cafeteria, that adds up to 4 ounces
of intestinal gas. That's a cloud of gas
the size of a small balloon.

over
1
quart of blood

A third of all the blood in your body circulates through your kidneys every minute (that's more than a quart). By the end of the day, they've filtered 190 quarts of blood.

And your kidneys help you eliminate 3 pints of urine every day. That breaks down to .03 of an ounce every minute—but "nature" doesn't call every minute . . .

Thank goodness!

70 to 120
heartbeats

If you're around 10 years old, your heart beats
between 70 and 120 times every minute, and faster
when you're exercising. If you're a newborn baby,
your heart is beating 100 to 200 times per minute
(and you probably can't read this book yet!).

When it comes to heartbeats, older means slower. Adult hearts beat anywhere
from 60 to 100 times per minute. And a well-exercised heart beats slower, as well:
Top athletes can have resting heartbeats as low as even 40 beats per minute!

Pump It Up!

Time to check your own heart's rate by taking your pulse. A simple method is to press your index finger against the hollow space right below where your thumb connects to your wrist. There's an artery close to the surface there. Once you can feel the soft throbbing pulse, **flip over your timer, and count the beats**.

To take your resting heart rate, first sit quietly for about ten minutes. Even better, check it in bed, just when you wake up.

Then compare your resting heart rate to your heart's rate after you've run full speed for several minutes. How much faster is it beating?

Your heart's maximum rate is easy to calculate: Just subtract your age from 220. Doctors and trainers say to exercise so that your heart beats at 65%–85% of its maximum rate.

GET OUT YOUR MINUTE GLASS

THE 60-SECOND ENCYCLOPEDIA

1,260
humming heartbeats

The human heart rate isn't shared by the rest of the animals in the kingdom. From the heart of the hibernating arctic ground squirrel (only 5 beats per minute) to the hummingbird heart (at 1,260 beats per minute, it's the fastest), each creature on the planet marches to the beat of its own heart.

We humans *do* share a pulse rate with two animals: the tickers inside cows and goldfish also happen to beat 70 times per minute.

207
THE 60-SECOND ENCYCLOPEDIA

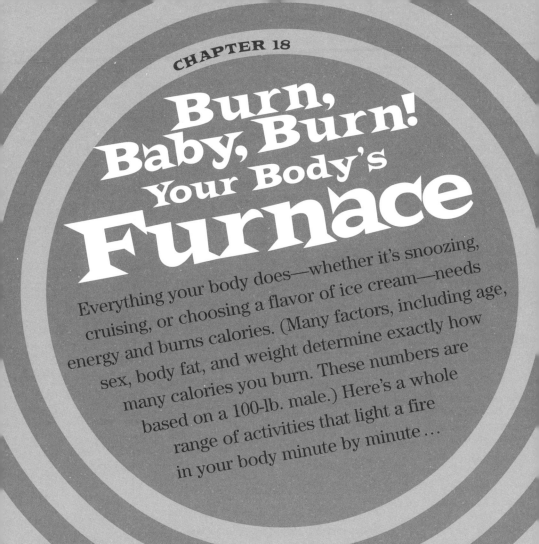

CHAPTER 18

Burn, Baby, Burn! Your Body's Furnace

Everything your body does—whether it's snoozing, cruising, or choosing a flavor of ice cream—needs energy and burns calories. (Many factors, including age, sex, body fat, and weight determine exactly how many calories you burn. These numbers are based on a 100-lb. male.) Here's a whole range of activities that light a fire in your body minute by minute...

1
resting-and-relaxing calorie

You'll burn only 1 calorie (or less) in a minute of sending e-mail, eating pancakes, watching cartoons, shuffling cards, or reading this book. Most sitting-down actions don't really get the old heart pumping.

If you're the average American kid, this year you'll spend 54,000 minutes sitting in school and 61,380 minutes sitting in front of a television. What's wrong with this picture . . .

209
THE 60-SECOND ENCYCLOPEDIA

3

let's-get-moving calories

Working in the garden, a little weight lifting,
a friendly game of volleyball, or most other mild exercises
will turn up your body's furnace by a few degrees.

What *is* a calorie? It's just a measure of energy. The more calories
you take in (also known as chowing down), the more energy
(also known as go-power) you can produce.

4
sort-of-sweating calories

That's what you burn when you're hiking, skateboarding, treading water, playing softball, or walking fast, like when you're hurrying around a swimming pool but don't want to get in trouble with the lifeguard ("*Tweeet!* No running!").

Statistically speaking, scientists have determined that every minute
you spend walking will extend your life by 2 minutes! So stay on that treadmill!
On the flip side, every cigarette you smoke cuts your life short by 11 minutes.

5

work-that-body! calories

You burn close to 5 whole calories when you're dancing fast, weight lifting like you mean business, downhill skiing, wrestling, or shoveling snow by hand.

Manjit Singh from the U.K. holds many records, including "139 Parallel Bar Dips in 1 Minute." In a single minute he can also stab 90 peas, 60 beans, or 65 kernels of corn with a toothpick and eat them one by one. Not the fastest way to fuel up!

Let's Have a Pick-nic!

Forks might be more efficient utensils for eating than a toothpick, but that's what you'll need to challenge Mr. Singh's record from the previous page. Grab your timer, a toothpick, and anything small and edible that can be speared: baked beans, peas, corn, blueberries, or, for a real challenge, cooked rice.

Flip over the timer, and **see how many individual bits you can harpoon, bring to your lips, and eat in a minute**.

This is a fun contest to try with friends all competing at the same time. (Laughing, however, is unlikely to increase your speed or efficiency.)

Bonus: Try this same challenge with two chopsticks.

GET OUT YOUR MINUTE GLASS!

6
pushing-hard calories

Rollerblading, hockey (both ice and field), jogging, playing tennis, and cross-country skiing burn about 6 calories each minute.

Obviously, it depends on how hard you play, right? You'll burn more calories in a brutal game of Ping-Pong than you will in a game of tennis doubles where you let your partner whack the majority of the balls.

7
heart-racing calories

You burn around 7 calories every minute of
playing football, mountain biking, boxing,
or swimming laps at a vigorous pace.

How many calories do you burn chewing gum?
Only about ⅙ calorie per minute. That's why personal trainers
hang out at the gym machines and not the gumball machines.

215

THE 60-SECOND ENCYCLOPEDIA

8

insanely sweaty calories

You'll burn at least 8 calories every minute of
sprinting full speed, playing handball, bicycling
as fast as you can, or doing high-impact aerobics.
Don't forget the deodorant.

Before major competitions, athletes often "carb up" by eating starchy foods
loaded with carbohydrates. These foods, like pasta and potatoes, provide
a long, steady stream of calories, supplying the muscles with ready energy.

In the Water!

Everybody in the pool! Slip on your goggles, pull on a bathing cap, and take a plunge with some wonders of the watery world. The speed of most water creatures depends on:

1) the animal's age
2) the temperature of the water (warmer water usually means faster; frozen water usually means . . . well, you're stuck)
3) the creature's length (long tails are a big help).
   And now, a regatta of racers . . .

the racers:

A Sea horse	11 inches
Ian Thorpe	374 feet
A Bottlenose Dolphin	
A Submarine	
A Swordfish	

the distance:
(FEET / MILES)

0	500	1,000	1,50

IN THE WATER

"Splash! The sea horse is barely moving, but the dolphin and the submarine are neck-and-neck (or is that neck-and-periscope?). Our human swimmer might have posed a threat to the swordfish if he'd brought along a fishing rod, but after 60 seconds of super speedy swimming, the swordfish is ahead by a *nose* . . . and then some!"

1,936 feet

2,006 feet

1 mile

00	2,500	3,000	3,500	4,000	4,500	5,000

½
← mile

1
← mile

THE WINNER!!

A Swordfish!

The swordfish gets its name from its long, sword-like bill, and it's not only fast (60 mph), it's big! A fully-grown swordfish can weigh well over 1,000 pounds.

2ND PLACE:

A Submarine

The Russians invented a sub in the 1970s that could travel 51 mph—twice as fast as today's subs. Unfortunately, extreme speed really damaged the sub's hull, not a good idea when you're deep underwater.

3RD PLACE:

A Bottlenose Dolphin

Dolphins have to surface to breathe, which makes a long, deep sleep impossible. (Imagine if you had to climb out of bed and run to the kitchen for a glass of air each time you wanted to breathe!)

4TH PLACE:

Ian Thorpe

Ian's freestyle skills are impressive. Another amazing minute record: In 2004, Brendan Hansen broke the one-minute barrier—and the world record!—when he swam the 100 meter breaststroke in 59:30 seconds.

5TH PLACE:

A Sea horse

OK, the sea horse is slow. But let's give the little fish a break! A sea horse has tiny gill fins for a motor and a stiff, upright body that's not exactly streamlined.

Different Strokes

Next time you're at the swimming pool or the lake, **have someone time you for 1 minute while you do your best dog-paddling stroke**. If you have a dog who likes to swim, why not test your pal's minute speed as well. Who's the better dog-paddler?

Here's another challenge for you: Measure the distance you travel in one minute of swimming your fastest front crawl (also known as the freestyle). After you catch your breath, put on a pair of swim fins, and repeat your freestyle sprint. How much further did you go? That fin power is the reason dolphins, whales, and fish can swim so fast without any arms!

GET OUT YOUR MINUTE GLASS

A Water Strider, at
294 feet

Water striders, also known as "pond skaters," can literally walk on water! Their bodies and legs are coated in thousands of tiny water-repellent hairs, and they weigh hardly anything. Because of these two physical attributes, a water strider doesn't break the surface tension of the water, and it can glide up to 294 feet in a minute.

Water striders stand on the surface of the water the way you'd stand on an enormous trampoline (minus the fun bouncing); their weight dents the surface, but they don't sink through, get wet, or even need a life jacket. So, these nifty bugs just don't belong in our swimming competition.

THE 60-SECOND ENCYCLOPEDIA

CHAPTER 19

Speedy Reading

Books, newspapers, comics, Web sites, fortune cookies, instructions, quizzes, signs—your day is crammed with things to read. (You're even reading right now!) But before you can read something, someone has to write it first. So every minute is filled with writers (*hello!*) and readers (that's you!). You could say the world is crawling with all of us bookworms!

250

words

The average person reads 250–300 words in a minute. If you're reading "heavier stuff," like a boring, complicated textbook, your speed will drop to 100 words per minute. If you're reading your little sister's ABC book, you'll probably zip through that entire book in a minute!

If you read braille, the alphabetical system of raised bumps that visually impaired people read with their fingertips, you take in about 125 words in a minute.

3,850 words!

The world record speed-reader, Sean Adam, can blast through a book at 3,850 words in a minute. Sean would have finished *this* book while you were still peeling the price sticker off the cover.

"Buddy, you were going 3,850 in a 250-word reading zone!"

4,756

cookbooks, mysteries, novels, travel guides . . .

Americans buy about 4,756 books every minute, for a total of nearly 7 million books every day. It's not that readers have to worry about running out of books to read: Approximately 479 new books are published each day.

Potter of Gold! 3,472 copies of *Harry Potter and the Order of the Phoenix* were sold every minute in the first 24 hours of its release—that's 5 million copies in one day!

Ready to Read?

The next two pages contain exactly 250 words, the average number of words someone reads in a minute. How does your reading rate compare?

Once you turn the page, **flip over the minute glass, and read along just the way you've been reading this book**. If you finish the page before the minute's up, go to the top and start over. When your minute's up, count the number of words you've read, including any words you read a second time.

Now, remember, you actually have to read the words, not just move your eyes back and forth across the lines. (There's even a little quiz following the article to test your comprehension.) But don't read aloud— that's a different test that comes later.

Ready, set, turn the page and flip your glass . . .

Some people—let's call them minute-maniacs—squeeze a little extra into a single minute. You might call this first gentleman a "news *breaker*!" Jean-Yves Mulot is an internationally known jujitsu guru and all-around daredevil. Not content with merely holding the world record for walking barefoot over sharp (48) axes—while blindfolded!—and obviously not interested in doing something more productive with all those axes like offering to help cut up some of the fallen trees in the neighborhood, this man broke, *in a single minute*, with one bare hand, 42 flame-covered, concrete blocks *and* another world record. (What the world record (101) was doing in that stack of blocks, no one knows.)

Let's call this second newsmaker "spellbinding!" The "world's fastest hypnotist" David Knight holds the record for hypnotizing 37 people *in less than a single minute*. He claims to have hypnotized more people than anyone else alive: (147) over 20,000 individuals. (Actually, GameCubes have hypnotized more people, according to the National Council of Parents Who Are Annoyed that Their Kids Won't Look Up from Their Games). The hypnotized volunteers started off standing, fully conscious, and then, within 60 seconds, they were all lying down like zombies, in what scientists call a "deep cataleptic trance state" (a form of unconsciousness where a person's muscles go rigid). To prove that the hypnotized individuals were not faking, scientific tests were used—more rigorous tests than the ones your mom uses when deciding if she should drag you out of bed from your pretend sleep. (250)

A 60-second Quiz

Reading fast is only useful if you absorb the content of what you've read. Let's see what you learned in our 250-word sample pages. Which, if any, of the following statements are true? *(The answers are on page 232.)*

1. David Knight hypnotized 20,000 people in 1 minute.

2. A deep cataleptic trance is when you fake being asleep.

3. GameCubes cause parents to put on blindfolds and go barefoot.

4. Never walk across sharp axes unless you've been hypnotized.

5. David Knight is the world's fastest zombie.

6. No, *you* are the world's fastest zombie.

7. Let me finish reading this book and forget about these minute-maniacs.

Sunday newspapers are even more popular: Sixty million copies sell each weekend.

680,555
Tribunes, Heralds, Times, and Posts

Every weekday (Monday through Friday), about 56 million newspapers are sold in the United States. Most adults spend 17½ minutes reading the newspaper each day, so that means that every minute, 680,555 newspapers are being read.

1,500
newspapers,
hot off the press!

Most newspapers are produced on printing presses
that are at least two stories tall. They can feed
nearly 2,500 feet of paper into the press and print 1,500
complete newspapers, complete with coupons, cartoons,
and movie listings, in a single minute.

Want another reason to recycle?
It takes the pulp of 500,000 trees to make all the Sunday papers.

20

pen-and-penciled words

Using a pen or pencil and just jotting down thoughts
from your own imagination or memory, the typical young
person writes about 20 words in a minute.

In the time it takes you to handwrite a single page (about 250 words),
you can read 12½ pages. How long it takes someone to read your
handwriting is an entirely different problem.

40

typewritten words

The typical typist, using both thumbs and all eight other fingers, can hammer out 40 words per minute. If you prefer the "hunt-and-peck" method (typing with just your two pointer fingers), you might poke out 10 words per minute.

Tip-top typists can more than double that average typing speed. Their flying fingers type 100 or more words in a minute—5 times the speed of handwriting.

Pangramania!

A pangram is a short sentence that uses all the letters of the alphabet at least once; they're great for practice typing. Sit at a computer or typewriter, flip over your minute glass, and **see how many of these pangrams you can type in 60 seconds**.

- The quiet zebra, mistaken for wearing convict clothes, expects to land in jail.

- Chefs made quick, inexpensive dinners just by microwaving frozen vegetables.

- Every king and queen just frowned at President Lincoln's amazing saxophone band.

- Inevitably, a dozen codfish eggs will make a quart of peach Jell-O extra salty.

- The busy aardvark sneezed whenever she pushed the just-fixed vacuum along the floor.

CHAPTER 20

Lift Your Voice

The typical gal speaks twice as many words per day as the typical guy! Does that sound about right to you? Maybe you're more of a motormouth. Maybe your lips are sealed. In either case, life's minutes are filled with the words, songs, and other noises that pipe up from our vocal cords . . .

163
chatty words

Your average speaking rate ranges from 150 to 175 words per minute during a typical conversation, so 163 words falls right in the middle. You tend to speak faster if you're nervous or excited, and slower if you're tired or arguing.

Every minute of speaking will spray an average of 300 droplets of water.
Cover your mouth and say, "Gross."

GET OUT YOUR MINUTE GLASS

Tongue-Tied Time Trial!

When you're talking tongue twisters, every word is a potential stumbling block! Do you have the Pronouncing Power to properly plow through this list of popular tongue twisters? **Flip over your minute glass, and say each tongue-tangling sentence correctly before moving to the next one.** Can you say them all in a minute? Challenge your friends to a contest, and see whose mouth muffs up the most.

- A giggling girl-gargoyle and a gargling guy-gargoyle got globs of gargantuan lollypops.
- Surely the Sugar Shack's salt shakers shouldn't serve sifted confectioners' sugar.

- Buoy noise annoys an innocent oyster. "They're selfish seashells"—so say some shrimp.

- Tiny Tim's the thin tinsmith's twin from Thistle, Smith, & Thimble, the three theatrical attorneys in town.

- Which wishy-washy witch switched one shaggy wig which wasn't wash 'n' wear?

- The sheik's sixth sense says his sheared sheep's still sick. Should the sheep seek shelter? Should the sheik seek a checkup for ticks?

- I'm missing my box of mixed biscuits, my messy biscuit mixer, and my proper copper coffee pot.

Biggest Bonus Bonanza:
Suppose you compose some impossibly compound prose, edit it a bit, and fuse a few user-confusing bursts of blubbering to flub up your friends. (In other words, make up your own tongue-twisters!)

160
words in your ear

When you're listening to someone tell a story, it's pretty comfortable to hear 160 to 175 words in a minute. Audio books are usually recorded at this rate.

"Going-once-going-twice-sold!" Auctioneers speak around 250 or more words per minute.

637
words whizzing past

The loquacious Steve Woodmore can speak 637 words in a
minute without gurgling—oops, that's *garbling* the words.
He's the record-holding speed-speaker.

Other notable fast talkers: President John F. Kennedy was one of the fastest public
speakers in history; he could speak over 300 words in a minute. And rapper Rebel
XD can utter more than 683 syllables in a hip-hop minute.

what your country can do for you . . .

"Wow!
That's <u>loco</u>
loquacious!"

"Ask not

241

160
barks

Dogs don't need a movie's special effects to make them talk. They're perfectly happy speaking in barks! During bird-hunting trials, a Finnish spitz (a reddish dog that looks like a fox/chow chow combo) is supposed to make 160 barks in a minute when it finds a bird in a tree.

42,000
echolocating clicks

When you're deep underwater, it's pretty dark,
and eyes aren't very useful. Hearing is! Dolphins "see"
underwater by *echolocation*: sending clicks into the water,
which bounce off objects (just like humans use radar).
In 1 minute, a dolphin can send, receive,
and process up to 42,000 clicks.

Did you
know that bats use
echolocation too? A bat
makes 12,000 clicks
per minute.

243
THE 60-SECOND ENCYCLOPEDIA

740

notes of a songbird

Some birds can sing 1,800 notes in a minute, but those songs are often monotonous: "la, la, la, la, la, etc." The European wren can sing 740 *different* notes in a minute: "do re mi fa sol la ti do!"

And it's loud! The European wren can be heard 500 meters away. Considering its tiny size, this is as if a human could sing loud enough to be heard 5 miles away.

1,320
yodeling notes

In 1992, the world's fastest yodeler, Thomas Scholl, yodeled 22 tones (15 falsetto) in 1 second. If he kept that up for an entire minute, he'd sing an incredible 1,320 notes—unless he choked on his Ricola cough drop.

The record for the fewest notes per minute is held by composer John Cage. His musical composition from 1952 titled *4'33"*, written "for any instrument," contains no notes at all— the performer just sits in silence on the stage for 4 minutes and 33 seconds!

CHAPTER 21

Hello?
Hello?

There are more than a few ways to "phone home" these days: home telephones, pay phones, cell phones, e-mail accounts, text messages, pagers, delivery services, "snail" mail—and new forms of communication are being invented all the time. You're "on call" no matter what the hour, no matter where you go. Each minute, millions and millions of people are staying in touch . . .

2,083,333
phone calls

Over 2 million phones are ringing every minute
in homes across the United States. Doctor's appointments,
carpool arrangements, catching up with old friends,
complaining about homework . . .

Before the invention of the telephone, there was
the telegraph. The fastest trained Morse code
officers could transmit 40–50 words per minute.

247

247

cell phones tossed out

More than 150 million Americans now own cellular phones. With each innovation (customized ring tones! mini-cameras!), people upgrade to new phones. Experts estimate that 130 million "old" cell phones are thrown out every year: 247 phones every minute!

Speaking of "throwing out" phones, folks in Finland hold the annual Mobile Phone Throwing World Championships. The 2004 winner, Ville Piippo, tossed a phone 271 feet.

Re: re: fwd:
21,527,777
e-mails

Over 21 million e-mails fly through cyberspace every minute. And this number is getting bigger and bigger all the time.

You've got mail! Unfortunately some of it is "spam."

Some authorities say 2 out of every 5 e-mails sent is junk. A good spam-blocking program helps you avoid this problem.

138,889
Google searches

The all-powerful search engine Google is powered by a bank of computers that scan some 3 billion Web pages more than 200 million times in a day. It performs 138,889 Internet searches each minute; each search takes only a fraction of a second.

Meanwhile, at least 1,400 new pages are uploaded to the World Wide Web every minute.

Surfing the Web

You and your computer are a team, like a horse and its jockey. (You decide which one you are.) Below are 3 searches; see if you can find the answers to each one in 1 minute! Use any computer with Internet access and any search engine you like (www.google.com is easy to use). **Flip over your minute glass, type the words that are in bold** (the quotation marks, too) into the computer's search window, then look among the sites that it finds for the answer. (*Answers are on page 253.*)

1. The Boston **"Red Sox" traded Babe Ruth** in what year?
2. **"J.K."** Rowling writes the **"Harry Potter"** books. What do her **initials "stand for"**?
3. In all of the **"Star Wars"** movies, who provides the **voice** of **C-3PO**?

207,947
pieces of stamped mail

Even with the billions of e-mails Americans send all year, 207,947 pieces of mail—letters, postcards, birthday invitations, and bills—pass through the U.S. Postal Service every minute! And that's not even counting junk mail.

The postal service is the second largest employer in the United States, and owns the biggest fleet of vehicles in the country. And if you tell any of its employees that you're a fan of "philately," they'll know you enjoy stamp collecting!

IN EVERY MINUTE OF SPEEDY DELIVERY . . .

2,147
packages

The U.S. Postal Service delivers over 2,147 packages each minute worldwide. (You didn't get a package today? Then think about writing more thank-you notes.)

UPS delivers 9,188 packages each minute, and FedEx delivers 3,819 packages a minute. These companies are the U.S. Postal Service's main competition!

Finding the Time

Every day, you hear people say "How do you find the time?" or "I just can't find the time!" Huh? Minutes aren't hiding! They're everywhere, even when you're not looking for them! Aside from clocks and wristwatches, there are lots of other devices tracking each 60 seconds.

- Is there a time blinking on your VCR, or tucked into the corner of your TV, or floating in the menu bar of your computer? The stove, coffeemaker, camera, stereo, MP3 player, thermostat, and many other electronic devices are ticking away as if their *real* job was to give you minute-by-minute updates (and, oh, as a bonus, also bake muffins or play CDs).

- How about the smoke alarm that beeps once a minute to tell you the battery is low? Or the microwave that beeps once a minute to tell you your food is ready? Are there sirens in your neighborhood that broadcast for a minute every Wednesday at exactly noon? And don't forget about those annoying one-minute Emergency Broadcast System tests that pop up on TV and the radio.

- And what about those minutes that are literally time-stamped on your belongings? Is there a bottling date on your milk carton or cup

of yogurt? The time is *ka-chunked* on the ticket that's ejected from the machine at the entrance to the parking garage.

• Your computer logs all your files and e-mails with a time "stamp." The phone company keeps track of the minutes you're gabbing on the phone. The power company makes sure each minute of electrical use at your house gets paid for.

You don't have to find the time— time finds you!

171,915
pieces of junk mail

Over 170,000 pieces of junk mail are delivered every minute: advertisements, catalogues, coupons that "you can't refuse" (but you do!). And, what's even worse, over 75,000 pieces of that junk mail are thrown away *unopened* every minute.

Be extra nice to your mail carrier. He or she delivers 2,300 pieces of mail every day to about 500 addresses, either on foot or in a U.S. Postal Service vehicle.

THE 60-SECOND ENCYCLOPEDIA

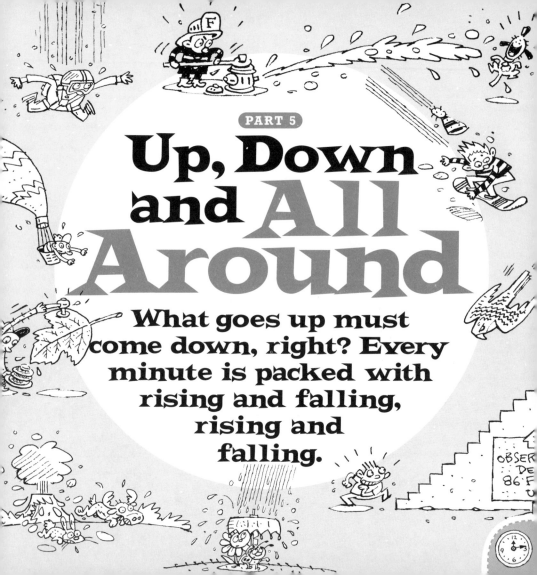

PART 5

Up, Down and All Around

What goes up must come down, right? Every minute is packed with rising and falling, rising and falling.

CHAPTER 22

Going with the FLOW

Did you know that the slowest flowing thing on Earth is . . . Earth? That's right: The planet we're standing on is moving. Feel it? (No? That's good. Unless you're in an earthquake, you're not supposed to—Earth's plates usually move just a few inches per year.) And every minute, there are all kinds of liquids slurping and sloshing along on this watery world of ours . . .

150
sappy drops

A big, old maple tree is full of the sap used to make maple syrup. During the peak 2 to 3 weeks of maple-sugaring time, about 150 drops will flow into a bucket every minute.

The sap that makes maple syrup is clear as water and only the slightest bit sweet. 30–40 gallons of sap are boiled down to create that 1 gallon of syrup that makes your pancakes taste delicious.

259
THE 60-SECOND ENCYCLOPEDIA

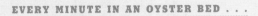

2

ounces of filtered water

A single oyster can filter more than 2 ounces of water
every minute, for around 30 gallons every day.
(A typical bathtub, filled to the brim, holds 50 gallons—
but no oysters.) These little bivalves suck in and squirt
out water, keeping the tiny bits of food they find.

In the Chesapeake Bay of a few hundred years ago, there were enough oysters to filter all the water in the bay—about 19 trillion gallons—in 3 to 6 days. Today, because of pollution and overharvesting, the remaining oysters would need more than 365 days to filter all the water in the bay.

ACME
50 GALLON TUB

The Famous Ketchup Challenge

Ketchup is a pretty slow flow-er, but is it faster than mustard? It's a condiment competition, so place your bets!

Apply a sample tablespoon of ketchup at one end of a "race track" (a cookie sheet) and a tablespoon of mustard next to it. **Flip over your timer, lift the starting end of your track about 5 inches** (leaving the other end down), and let the flow go go go! When the minute is up, take a ruler and measure the distance your racers traveled: Those are their flow rates, measured in inches per minute. Did you predict the winner?

You can race all your favorite condiments: syrup, fudge sauce, cocktail sauce. Just be sure to ask permission before you start raiding the fridge for contestants.

GET OUT YOUR MINUTE GLASS !

Assuming that these colossal guys are as tasty as they are large, one 1,400-pound pumpkin can make about 700 pies.

EVERY MINUTE IN THE PUMPKIN PATCH . . .

1
liter of water
for a jack-o-lantern

All plants need water to survive—even a cactus!
But a world-class gargantuan pumpkin, weighing 500
to nearly 1,400 pounds, drinks about 1 liter of water every
minute, and it uses every drop; these pumpkins can pack
on up to 30 pounds in 24 hours!

3 1/5
cups of milk

Milking machines can "extract" 3 or more cups of milk from a cow in 1 minute, for a typical total of 8 gallons of milk each day. (It takes approximately 340–350 squirts to obtain just 1 gallon of milk.)

When cows listen to soothing music, they'll produce about 3 more cups of milk a day compared to when there's nothing but barnyard mooing.

264

THE 60-SECOND ENCYCLOPEDIA

3

hot 'n' tired gallons of water

Now a camel that is thirsty (maybe it's been hiking through the desert for 8 straight days without a drink— *and a camel can!*) will drink 3 gallons of water in 1 minute. Ten minutes and as much as 30 gallons later— that's enough liquid to fill the gas tank of a super-cab pickup truck—the camel will feel refreshed.

Does the camel's hump hold all that water? No, it stores the fat that provides the energy for the camel on those long, hot journeys.

THE 60-SECOND ENCYCLOPEDIA

5

gallons of sudsy water

Your daily shower uses 4 or 5 gallons of water every minute. But, if your house has a water-conserving showerhead (a good idea!), you save water, using only 2½ gallons per minute.

An elephant showers itself with water, too, to keep cool. Its trunk can hold 2 gallons of water at once.

What's Your Flow?

GET OUT YOUR MINUTE GLASS!

This is a good challenge for a hot day, because things are about to get wet! Which has a faster flow rate: your bathtub or your kitchen sink? Grab a 5-gallon bucket, a measuring cup, and your minute glass to find out.

Hold your bucket under your bathtub spigot, **flip the minute glass, and let 'er rip, full blast, until the minute runs out.** Then measure how much water is in the bucket to find your rate of flow in gallons per minute.

Once you've recorded the amount, use the water to give your plants and hedges a drink or to scrub your kitchen floor (right!), and then repeat the activity for your kitchen sink faucet and maybe even your garden hose.

A leaky faucet that drips 120 times in a minute—merely 2 teaspoons—will add up to 15 gallons of water in a day.

1,000
gushing gallons
of water

A fire hydrant releases 1,000 gallons of water in a minute.
Some fire departments have special sprinkler caps
to put on fire hydrants to reduce the gushing
flow to 25 gallons per minute so that kids can cool off
in the spray on hot summer days. Whee!

When firefighters respond to a house fire, their crosslay hoses can shoot
100 gallons of water per minute.

2½
miles of volcanic debris

In 1980, Washington State's 40,000-year-old volcano, Mount St. Helens, erupted. The eruption was so powerful that it sent an avalanche of debris flowing at a speed of 2½ miles per minute, or 150 miles per hour— definitely some of the fastest-moving land on Earth.

The biggest volcano in the solar system happens to be on Mars. Named Olympus Mons, it's more than 8 times taller than Mount St. Helens ever was!

4,722,222
gallons of fresh water

All around the world, some 13,600 freshwater "factories" remove salt from saltwater (a process called desalination). They pump out 4,722,222 gallons of brand-new freshwater in a minute (6.8 billion gallons every day).

This amazing minute's worth of desalination would flood a football field to the height of more than 11 feet of fresh water, taller than the goalpost's crossbar!

900,000
gallons of
Big Apple water

It takes a lot of water to wash an apple the size of Manhattan. The largest city in the United States, New York City uses more than 900,000 gallons of water every minute.

CHAPTER 23

Everything that Rises ...

You *rise* from bed each morning. Dough *rises*. Crowds at a concert *rise* to their feet. Temperatures *rise*. The hairs on the back of your neck *rise* when you're scared or chilly. Every minute, thousands of things—and people!—defy the law of gravity ... or *fly* trying!

165
stair-climbing steps

The fastest man to run up the Empire State Building,
Paul Crake, bounded up 165 steps every minute to
climb the building's 1,576 steps and 86 floors in
less than 10 minutes.

Mr. Crake's "taking the
stairs" hardly compares
with taking the elevator.
Its speed is more than
12 times faster, rising
1,400 feet in a
minute.

OBSERVATION
DECK
86 FLOORS
UP

The Empire State Building Challenge!

Think you're up for this stair-climbing feat? Running up stairs is a bigger calorie burner than walking or even jogging— even in the comfort of your own home.

Choose a staircase (preferably one with a good handrail, in case you lose your balance). Count the number of steps. Then flip over your minute glass and **see how many steps you can climb up and down before the sand runs out**.

Then divide the Empire State Building's 1,576 steps by the number of steps you climbed. That's how many minutes it would take you to reach the top of the building. How do you compare to our record holder? And remember, he was climbing *up* 100% of the time.

880

jet-propelled feet into the air

Go 007! James Bond's jet pack, in the 1965 movie
Thunderball, rocketed him through the air
at 616 to 880 feet per minute
(a mere 7 to 10 miles per hour).

The jet pack was real, not a
special effect! Unfortunately,
it didn't go very high and only
lasted 30 seconds.

293
frigid feet into the air

On its way to the stars, a helium balloon floats upward
293 feet each minute. But after 90 minutes or so,
at a height of about 5 miles, it pops!

It's cold up there (well below 0°F), and the balloon's rubber gets brittle and cracks.

If you
were up here you'd
turn into a big
icicle!

792
windblown feet

Unless a tremendous breeze happens to spring up,
a hot-air balloon drifts through the air, traveling around
792 feet in a minute (about 9 miles per hour).

Most hot-air balloons carry 30 gallons of propane in their tanks,
enough to power 6 huge outdoor grills for hours of cookout fun!

880

feet up the mountaintop

There's an ultramodern gondola lift in Lake Tahoe, California, which shuttles skiers two miles up the mountain at a rate of 880 feet each minute.

It takes about 12 minutes to reach the top of the mountain. Even if you don't ski, the view is out-of-this-world!

279

THE 60-SECOND ENCYCLOPEDIA

Are All Minutes Created Equal?

Yes, even though that provision was left out of the Declaration of
Independence. All minutes are 60 seconds, even though there are
moments when time seems to be passing far too quickly—
or way too slowly. Do the items in these lists *ring a bell?*

Minutes Seem Too Short When You're . . .

• sledding or skiing down a hill, or skating down a ramp.

• watching the Fourth of July fireworks display, which are over before
you know it.

• up to bat at the plate and the bases are loaded and—*STEEE-RIKE!*

• wishing you could stay in bed for just five more minutes, *just a few
more minutes, please!*

• taking turns on the trampoline or
the dirt bike or anything else you
have to share.

• in the middle of your best round
yet of *The Sims* or *Madden NFL*,
when you're really concentrating.

Minutes Seem To Take Forever When You're . . .

• waiting in the waiting room of the doctor's office . . .

• trying to fall asleep and the pillow is too crunchy and it's getting later and later . . .

• sitting on the bench waiting for the coach to put you in the game . . .

• walking home with your heavy, heavy backpack and it's making your back sweat because it's hot and you're not even halfway there . . .

• late and you're stuck in the car on the way to school behind a trash truck in a lot of traffic . . .

• OW! You just bumped your head or banged your elbow and the pain is overwhelming (even though you know it's going to pass eventually) . . .

• you're bored and hungry and you have plenty of time to think about how there's nothing fun to do and there's never any good food in the house . . .

60

planes take off

Speaking of liftoffs, every minute, an average of 60 propeller and jet planes are taking off or landing in the United States. During peak air travel times, there are between 4,000 and 6,000 airplanes flying every hour.

Chicago's O'Hare Airport is the busiest in the world.
Every minute, 1 or 2 flights take off.

In the Air!

Most things that fly are fast. It's just one of gravity's rules: If you want to get off the ground, well, you've got to spend a whole lot of energy flapping. Without enough speed, you're simply grounded. Here's a high-flying race featuring our aerial competitors . . .

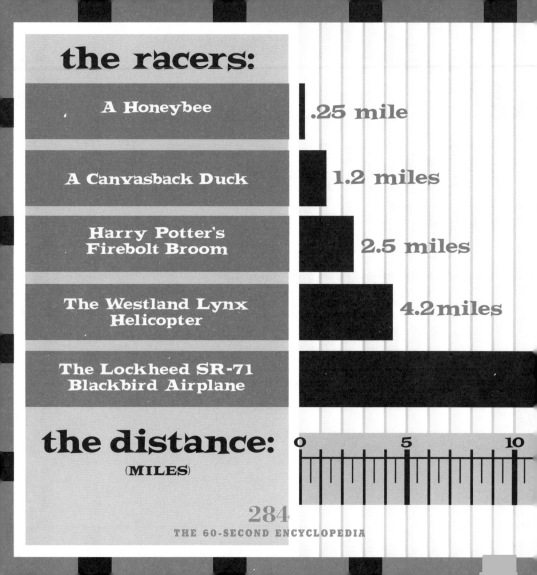

the racers:

A Honeybee — .25 mile

A Canvasback Duck — 1.2 miles

Harry Potter's Firebolt Broom — 2.5 miles

The Westland Lynx Helicopter — 4.2 miles

The Lockheed SR-71 Blackbird Airplane

the distance:
(MILES)

0   5   10

IN THE AIR

"And they're off! The airplane takes off to an early lead. The honeybee seems to be taking its *sweet* time, but the rest are racing into the wild blue yonder. The canvasback duck and Harry Potter on his Firebolt are flying along, but the machines are faster. After 60 seconds of fast flying, the Lockheed SR-71 Blackbird Airplane is the champion."

36.7 miles

15   20   25   30   35

A CLOSER LOOK AT OUR CONTESTANTS

THE WINNER!!

The Lockheed SR-71
Blackbird Airplane

This plane flies three times faster than the speed of sound. It can reach an altitude of 85,000 feet, so high that crew members wear pressurized suits (like astronauts).

2ND PLACE:

The Westland Lynx Helicopter

This is the fastest helicopter ever built. Not as fast as an airplane, the helicopter can do things planes can't, such as hover and fly backwards.

3RD PLACE:

Harry Potter's Firebolt Broom

Harry's a champion Quidditch player, thanks to his incredibly fast Firebolt broom, which can reach 150 mph. His old broom, the Nimbus 2000, was slower.

4TH PLACE:

A Canvasback Duck

This duck could outfly a kicked soccer ball (1.16 miles per minute or 70 miles per hour), but not a whacked hockey puck (1.67 miles per minute—more than 100 miles per hour).

5TH PLACE:

A Honeybee

In its entire life, one honeybee will make a mere $\frac{1}{12}$ teaspoon of honey— 5 drops! The next time you spread a tablespoon of honey on your biscuit, remember that it's the life work of 36 bees!

Take to the Air!

People have always longed to fly. And ever since that first flight by the Wright brothers over 100 years ago, air transportation has become a reality. But without a pilot's license and a private jet, you can't just take to the air whenever you're in the mood.

But you can send an "ambassador" into the sky for a minute! You'll need two inflated balloons (not helium!), a paper fan, and your minute glass. **Flip the minute glass and try to keep both balloons suspended in the air for 1 minute.** Can you provide lift power? If not, try using one balloon.

You can also use a stopwatch to see how long you can keep a paper airplane, a Frisbee, or a giant soap bubble floating up in the air. (Don't forget to serve peanuts and a choice of beverages!)

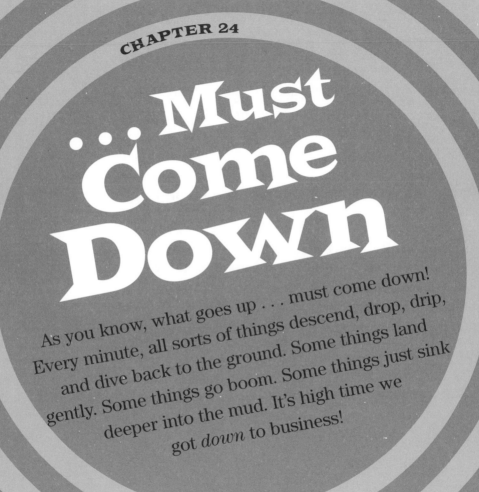

CHAPTER 24

...Must Come Down

As you know, what goes up . . . must come down! Every minute, all sorts of things descend, drop, drip, and dive back to the ground. Some things land gently. Some things go boom. Some things just sink deeper into the mud. It's high time we got *down* to business!

.0000047
inches down

Poor, gigantic, jam-packed Mexico City is sinking!
Every minute, it's 0.0000047 inches lower. That adds up—
or *down*—to 2½ inches each year, 27 total feet in the 20th
century. (Venice in Italy and our own Louisiana coast
are also sinking alarmingly fast.)

Mexico City is built on top of an underground
water reservoir. As the water gets
pumped up, the weight of all those
buildings and people pushes down
into the soggy, empty space. Talk
about a sinking feeling!

289

December 31's final

77

feet

The official New Year's Eve ball in New York City's Times Square drops 77 feet in its annual moment of fame and glory—the last minute of the old year—to proclaim "Happy New Year!"

The enormous crystal ball weighs 1,070 pounds.

You don't want to drop that on your toe.

11,038
snow-packed feet

Record-holding snowboarder Darren Powell careens down the slopes at just over 11,038 feet in a minute, or 125.45 miles per hour.

The speediest skiers are even faster! They fly down the slopes at a rate of 2.5 miles per minute (more than 150 miles per hour)!

291

THE 60-SECOND ENCYCLOPEDIA

2
free-falling miles

Before the parachute opens, a skydiver plummets through the air at a speed of just less than 2 miles per minute. That's the distance from the tops of many clouds to the Earth!

Once the parachute opens, the skydiver's speed drops to 1,000 feet in a minute (about 11 miles per hour) for a much softer landing.

This is our winner of winners, the fastest of the fastest: No other living thing on the planet can move at a greater speed.

DIVE BOMB AWARD

3⅓
dive-bombing miles

The peregrine falcon is the fastest diver of any creature on land, at sea, or in the air. When pursuing a bit of supper (a smaller bird), the falcon dive-bombs at a speed of 3⅓ miles per minute (200 miles per hour!).

CHAPTER 25

The Sky is Falling! The Sky is Falling!

"It's raining, it's pouring …" and all kinds of things are showering down on us that have nothing to do with "old men" and "snoring." Whether from a big, puffy cloud or an intergalactic storm, something's in the air.…

Heads up!

198

gently falling feet

A little raindrop in a gentle spring drizzle falls down at a speed of 198 feet a minute (that's about 2¼ miles an hour). And rain can fall a whole lot faster, too!

If you're caught in a rainstorm, are you drier if you run or walk to shelter? The answer according to meteorologists Thomas Peterson and Trevor Wallis is: Run! You'll still get wet, but as long as shelter is near, you'll be drier running than walking. (You'll be 100% drier if you just remember your umbrella!)

295

264
gracefully falling feet

In a minute, a snowflake travels down about 264 feet, slowly and gracefully (like a tiny, frozen parachute). Snowflakes are crystals that form when water vapor freezes.

Got snow? Ski resorts can improve their trails, using machines that turn thousands of gallons of water into snow every minute.

2
fast-and-furious miles

Hail weighs more than rain or snow, and it falls faster.
Small hail falls about a half a mile per minute, but when hail
reaches the size of golf balls (just under 1¾ inches in
diameter) it falls nearly 2 miles straight down in a minute.

The biggest hailstone ever found was 5.6 inches in diameter—
bigger than a softball!

Rain Gauge

Here's a rainy day activity: Use your minute glass to create a *pluviometer* (the official word for a rain gauge!). You'll need a ruler and a rain collector: any straight-sided, flat-bottomed vessel such as a cake pan or empty jar. If it's raining hard, you might want an umbrella, too.

Place your rain collector in the rain just as you flip over the timer and **let the rain accumulate until the sand runs out.** Then grab the rain collector and go someplace dry.

Insert the ruler into the accumulated water to measure the rate it's raining per minute. Unless it's really pouring, a minute's worth of rain is probably going to be a fraction of an inch. You can also collect rain for 10 minutes or for 1 hour, and divide the amount collected by the total number of minutes.

GET OUT
YOUR
MINUTE
GLASS

10 inches of snow melts into just one inch of rain. That snow is fluffy stuff!

2
inches of torrential rain

The fiercest downpour that has been recorded was in
Basse-Terre, Guadeloupe, on Nov. 26, 1970.
In a single minute, it rained nearly 2 inches.

2,916,666,667
gallons of precipitation

If you add up every drizzle, snowfall, hailstone,
and thunderstorm, the total precipitation that falls on
the United States in a day is about 4.2 trillion gallons.
That averages out to nearly 3 billion gallons of water
descending on the U.S. every minute.

But that rain isn't divided up equally! There's definitely more rain falling in states
like Florida, Hawaii, and Washington, and hardly any in Nevada and Arizona.

Sometimes
it's best to
stay inside!

Now that's one fat dust bunny!

.0012
ounces of house dust

Almost .0012 ounces of dust fall in your house each minute. That adds up to 40 pounds of dust in a year.

Forty pounds of dust weigh as much as 8 regular bags of flour. Flour also tends to "dust" the surfaces in your kitchen if you're a messy cook.

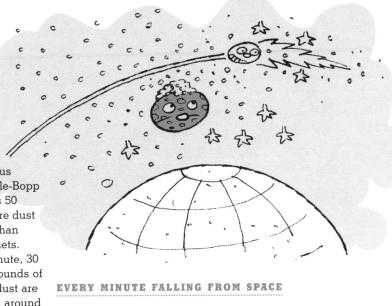

The famous comet Hale-Bopp generates 50 times more dust and gas than most comets. Every minute, 30 million pounds of gas and dust are vaporized around this chunk of ice and dust.

153
pounds of cosmic dust

Each day, between 55 and 110 tons of Milky Way powder, galactic grit, and other interstellar bits sprinkle down on us from the heavens. That's 76–153 pounds of cosmic dust each minute.

Set Your Clocks

So now that you've seen the sheer power of the minute, you probably want to make sure you're not missing out on a single one. But, horrors! Your watches and clocks could be fast, slow, or just blinking *12:00!*

Use the most accurate timing device in the world to set the clocks around your house: an atomic clock. This "timepiece" is about the size of a restaurant refrigerator, and it's based on a power source that won't wear out like a battery or break like a winding mechanism: an atom called cesium-133. Its measure of time is so accurate, that in 30 million years, this clock *might* lose one second of time; happily, we have quite a few years before we need to worry.

You can set your own clocks with this official atomic time clock by logging onto **www.time.gov**., which lists the official U.S. time in every time zone.

A World of Difference

Having read this entire book, you may feel that the minute is now your best friend. Or your *second*-best friend (ha!). But you might still wonder: "Are minutes THAT important, after all? Can't a person just be a little early or late? What difference do teensy bits of time really make?"

Well, there are plenty of businesses and industries that depend on incredibly precise timing to create global transportation schedules, electric power, manufacturing processes, communication signals, and both molecular and astronomical research. And here's one BIG example.

When a satellite in space is beaming signals, it's creating a three-dimensional picture by teaming up with the signals of other satellites. As their beams overlap, their two perspectives can pinpoint things with greater accuracy (similar to the way your eyes, aiming from two slightly different perspectives, accurately figure out the location of objects here on Earth). The space-based distances involved often span thousands of miles, meaning an error in a satellite's transmission of 1 billionth of 1 second (that's a *nanosecond*) creates a positioning miscalculation of 1 foot. It could mean your cell phone doesn't work or your satellite TV is all fuzzy. And if you're firing a rocket or landing an aircraft, that little error is critical. A mistake as big as an entire minute would be astronomical—a positioning miscalculation of hundreds or even thousands of miles. It could be a matter of life and death.

A minute can make a world of difference. And so can you. Spend your minutes here on Earth doing all the kind and generous things that you can. As you've seen, each minute has the power to accomplish the amazing.

About the Author

Michael J. Rosen, who is 26,298,000 minutes old as of this writing, is the author of 60 books. (No, he did not write one each minute for a total of one hour.) His books for young readers include *Kids' Best Dog Book* and *The Kids' Book of Fishing*, as well as picture books and young adult novels. He's also created many anthologies to benefit Share Our Strength's fight to end hunger and collections that support various animal welfare efforts throughout the country. A poet, cookbook author, and editor of the humor biennial *Mirth of a Nation*, Michael lives in central Ohio on an old farm with a lawn that takes 480 minutes to mow. His Web site is www.fidosopher.com.

Are Two Legs Better than Four?

Why do people walk on two legs instead of on all fours, anyway? Find a wide-open space suitable for running, because after this two-part race you'll know why!

First, measure how far you can run at your top speed for a single minute. (Let someone else hold the timer, so you're not shaking up the seconds of sand!) Mark your starting place as well as your finishing place.

Once you catch your breath, return to your starting place and get on all fours like a quadruped (four-legged animal) instead of a biped (two-legged animal). **Now see how far you can run using your hands and your feet**.

Chances are, your biped-self *smoked* your quadruped-self.

What's America Eating Every Minute?

Unlike grazing elephants or panda bears, humans eat only a few times a day: breakfast, lunch, dinner, and maybe a snack or two. But our country has nearly 300 million people spread out over 50 states and 6 different time zones, and the truth is that every minute of the day, millions of people are eating. So, based on yearly food consumption figures, here's a look at what our nation consumes in just one minute of eating:

Whether they're used for making omelets, egg-salad sandwiches, or homemade cakes, **144,995 large eggs** are cracked every minute. For other hungry people, **10,435 six oz. containers of yogurt** are scooped up and **5,208 Krispy Kreme® doughnuts** are devoured. And every minute, hungry eaters wash their meals down with **335,066 cups of coffee** and **over 20 tons of orange juice.**

Do you feel like chicken tonight? **29,305 pounds of chicken** are cooked and served up in chicken noodle soup, chicken salad, buckets of fried chicken, and chicken McNuggets. Every 60 seconds, seafood lovers consume **8,209 pounds of shrimp, crab, salmon, tuna, and other fish and shellfish.** Also on our collective plates, every minute we also consume **8,945 pounds of potato chips** and **6,414 pounds of pickles.** And just like mom says, people need to eat their vegetables: **2,298 pounds of broccoli** and **7,006 pounds of carrots** are crunched every minute.

And forget about dieting—there's plenty of dessert being eaten too. **9,121 pounds of ice cream** and **6,502 pounds of chocolate** are consumed every minute. (Did you say "Brownie Sundae?")

And this is just the tip of the iceberg. The truth is, in a country the size of America, enormous tons of food are consumed every single minute.

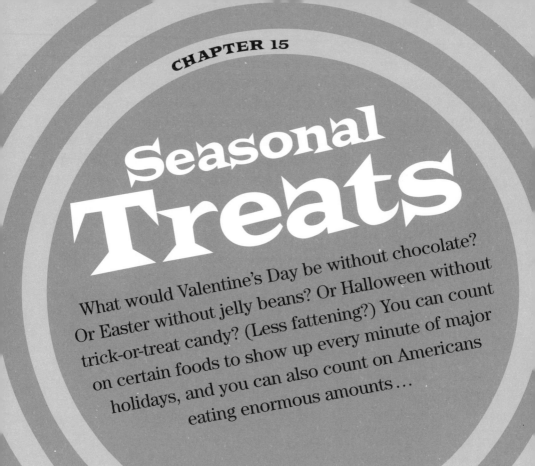

Seasonal Treats

What would Valentine's Day be without chocolate? Or Easter without jelly beans? Or Halloween without trick-or-treat candy? (Less fattening?) You can count on certain foods to show up every minute of major holidays, and you can also count on Americans eating enormous amounts ...

132,275
Sweethearts®
Conversation Heart candies

"Be Mine!" "2 Sweet!" Necco sells a total of 8 billion Conversation Heart candies during the 6 weeks between January 1 and February 14, Valentine's Day!

Conversation Hearts have been around since 1866. They used to be larger, with space for lovey-dovey thoughts such as "Please send a lock of your hair by return mail," and "How long shall I have to wait? Pray be considerate."

17,123
pieces of candy corn

Around Halloween, we eat 35 million total pounds of candy corn. Not that anyone's counting, but that's equivalent to 9 billion kernels of candy corn.

And in case you want to celebrate, October 30 is National Candy Corn Day.

104,166
hot dogs

Over 150 million hot dogs are sold on
the Fourth of July weekend alone. During the peak hours
of picnicking and partying, 104,166 hot dogs—
slathered in mustard, relish, sauerkraut, or chili—are slid
between buns and chomped every minute.

Every hot dog has its day—
not just the Fourth of July!
Over 24 million hot dogs are
sold at major league baseball
stadiums each season.

3,333
pizzas

Each minute of Super Bowl Sunday (the third biggest eating day of the year), Domino's® boxes up and delivers 3,333 pizza pies, for a total of 1.2 million halftime snacks. (That's figuring 6 hours of major pizza ordering surround the game.)

Some pizza makers are athletes too! They participate in international competitions in dough acrobatics, pizza skin stretching, and overall most delicious pizza.

174
THE 60-SECOND ENCYCLOPEDIA

Faster and Faster Fast Food

Every minute is money for fast-food restaurants. At the 6,500 Taco Bells® around the country, the goal is to have you order, pay, and drive off with your food in 1 minute. At the 6,513 Wendy's®, the drive-through greeting is supposed to take just 3 seconds.

Next time your family visits the drive-through to order a fast-food meal, flip over your minute glass. How many minutes do you spend waiting in line before you even place your order? How many minutes pass between the time you give your order and you drive off with your food? Start keeping a chart in the car to see which establishments provide the fastest service.

793,651
jelly beans

Around Easter, an average 793,651 jelly beans are eaten every minute . . . and that's assuming the Easter baskets' contents actually last for 2 weeks!

And every minute of Easter, 62,500 chocolate Easter bunnies hippity-hop out of Easter baskets and into people's stomachs.

12,220
snails

While you may eat turkey for Christmas dinner, folks in France are feasting on escargot (snails!). The French love snails, and they're extra-popular at Christmastime. Every minute, 12,200 snails are being sucked down, for a total of 22 tons of snails consumed in just one day.

Don't forget, May 24th is National Escargot Day!

95,833
turkeys

Almost 95,833 turkeys are served each minute in the
8 hours of Thanksgiving Day meals.

Of the 269 million turkeys sold each year, 45 million are part of that feast.

And make it snappy!

Why do you feel so sleepy after Thanksgiving dinner?
It could be the chemical L-tryptophan, found in turkey, which causes drowsiness . . .
or it could be just plain old overeating!

CHAPTER 16

Munching Madness

Maybe lions and dogs scarf down their dinners, but people are supposed to relax, eat slowly, and savor each meal. Well, some people didn't get that memo. Instead, they've perfected the art of pigging out! Here are record-holding chow-hounds and what they can eat in one minute . . . (Do *not* get out your minute glass to try any of these at home—or, in a restaurant!)

4½
hot dogs

Weighing a mere 132 pounds, Takeru Kobayashi of Japan holds the record for eating 53½ hot dogs in 12 minutes, which is almost 4½ hot dogs every minute!

In the doughnut (or just plain nuts!) category, Eric "Badlands" Booker holds the record: 6 doughnuts every minute for 8 minutes, totaling 49 doughnuts and a whopping stomachache.

10
jalapeño peppers

In the burning-hot category, Jed Donahue ate 10 jalapeño peppers—that's an extremely fiery pepper—every minute for 15 minutes in a row: a total of 152 peppers.

Brian Seiken scarfed down about half a pound of pickles per minute for a total of 6 minutes and over 2½ pounds of pickles.

ice cream scoops

Ed "Cookie" Jarvis treated himself to 6 ounces—
that's two scoops—of vanilla ice cream every minute for
a total of 12 minutes. That's a "snack" of 1 gallon plus
1½ cups of the frozen stuff.

Of course it gave
him an ice-cream
headache!

Doesn't it give
you one, just
reading about it?

9

eggs

How do you like your eggs: scrambled or fried?
Sonya Thomas must like hers hard-boiled;
she wolfed down 9 eggs per minute for a grand total of
65 hard-boiled eggs in 6 minutes and 40 seconds.

The recommended caloric intake for kids is around 2,000 calories per day
(or 1.4 calories per minute). 65 eggs contain a whopping total of 4,875 calories!

36
cockroaches

Ken Edwards of England ate 36 cockroaches
in a single minute, winning the distinction of, well,
eating 3 dozen cockroaches.

Was there a
congratulatory
kiss afterward?

Maybe not.

Polly Want a Cracker?

Time to take the *Great Saltine Challenge*. Here's all you'll need: your minute glass, 5 saltines (that's 5 cracker squares), and a glass of water that you can't drink until the contest is over. Yes, that's the challenge: You don't get anything to wash down the salty crumbs along the way.

Flip over the timer, and see how many saltines you can eat in 60 seconds. You have to swallow each cracker before starting on the next. You can't have any cracker in your mouth when the time's up—and some really crack-competitors say you even have to whistle (any tune that's not just a spray of cracker crumbs and spit is okay) to prove you've finished.

37
ounces of Jell-O®

In the wiggly food category, Steven M. Lakind
sucked down 37 ounces of Jell-O in a single minute
and continued to slurp it down for another 2 minutes.
His total Jell-O ingestion was nearly 112 ounces—
that's seven boxes worth!

During the early 20th century, immigrants arriving at Ellis Island in New York City
were served Jell-O as a "Welcome to America" meal.

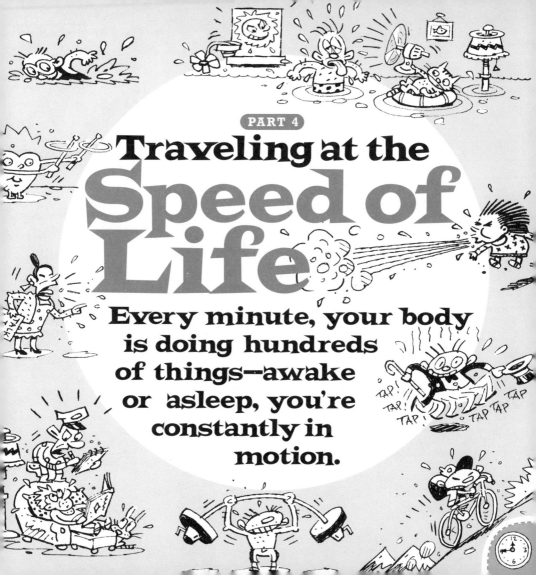

PART 4

Traveling at the Speed of Life

Every minute, your body is doing hundreds of things—awake or asleep, you're constantly in motion.

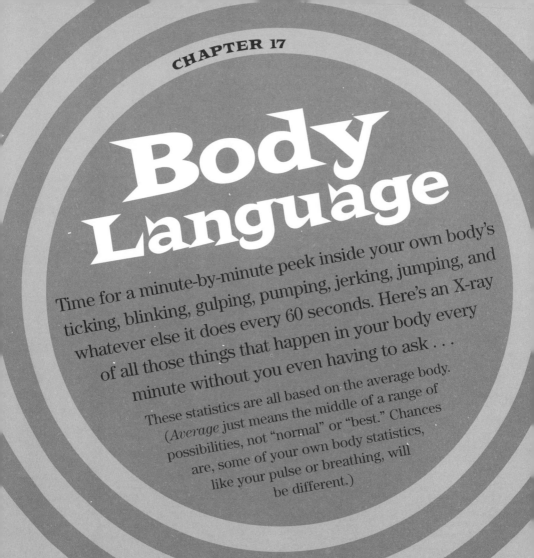

CHAPTER 17

Body Language

Time for a minute-by-minute peek inside your own body's ticking, blinking, gulping, pumping, jerking, jumping, and whatever else it does every 60 seconds. Here's an X-ray of all those things that happen in your body every minute without you even having to ask . . .

These statistics are all based on the average body. (*Average* just means the middle of a range of possibilities, not "normal" or "best." Chances are, some of your own body statistics, like your pulse or breathing, will be different.)

"In the blink of an eye . . ." The eyelid is the fastest contracting muscle in your body.

EVERY WATCHFUL MINUTE . . .

12 to 15
blinks per minute

That's the average. Add a few more blinks if you're nervous (25 times per minute). Subtract a few if you're concentrating, on the computer, or watching TV (7 times per minute).

The soft lights and mellow music in shopping malls slow your blinking as well . . . store owners want you to feel relaxed, and ready to spend!

Catching Some Blinks!

Your eyes blink all the time to keep your eyeballs clean and moistened. But you *can* control this reflex somewhat. Can you go an entire minute without blinking?

Flip over your minute glass and try not to blink for 1 entire minute. How do your eyes feel? (Blinking coats the surface of your eyes with tears, which has nothing to do with being sad.)

Now have a friend count how many times you blink. To get your "natural" rate of blinking, you shouldn't know when your blinks are being counted. Then observe the blinking rate of some of your friends, and see who's the blinking-est of your bunch.

.000018

inches of hair growth

And that's just too tiny to see with the naked eye!
There are about 120,000 hairs on your head, and each one
grows only .017 inches in a day—about ½ inch a month.

How long would it take you to grow Rapunzel-length hair? Even if her tower was
only 10 feet tall, that 10 feet of hair would take you at least 20 years to grow,
or more, since the longer it gets, the slower it grows.

8

swallowed drops of spit

Every minute, your body produces $\frac{1}{50}$ of an ounce of saliva (that's 8 drops), for a total of 4 cups of the stuff in a day.

You also swallow 1 or 2 times every minute even when you aren't eating. And when you're nervous, your body cranks out extra saliva, so you need to swallow more.